It's another Quality Book from CGP

Want to hear the **bad news**? There's an awful lot of tricky
technical stuff they expect you to learn for KS3 ICT.

Want to hear the **good news**? Good old CGP have got it all covered!
We've produced this brilliant book with all the "techy details"
beautifully explained in clear, simple English so you can understand it.

And then, in the spirit of going the extra mile, we've put some daft bits in to try
and make the whole experience at least vaguely entertaining for you.

We've done all we can — the rest is up to you.

What CGP is all about

Our sole aim here at CGP is to produce the highest quality
books — carefully written, immaculately presented and
dangerously close to being funny.

Then we work our socks off to get them out to you
— at the cheapest possible prices.

Contents

Section 1 — The Parts of a Computer System

Data 1
Computer Systems 2
Computerised v. Manual Systems 3
Network Security 4
Input Devices 5
Revision Summary for Section One 7

Section 2 — Using a Computer System

Data Capture 8
Data Capture — Form Design 9
Benefits and Problems of Data Collection 10
Data Storage and Processing 11
Data Presentation 12
Revision Summary for Section Two 13

Section 3 — Systems Analysis

Step One — Identify the Problem 14
Analysis — The Feasibility Study 15
Design — Input, Process, Output 16
Design — Flow Diagrams 17
Writing a Procedure 18
Revision Summary for Section Three 19

Section 4 — Text and Image Processing Software

Word Processing Basics 20
Word Processing — Advanced Features 22
Graphics — Creating Images 24
Changing the Images 25
Editing Digital Images 26
Desktop Publishing — Basics 27
DTP — Working with Frames 28
DTP — Producing a Newspaper 29
Presentation Software 30
Revision Summary for Section Four 32

Section 5 — Spreadsheets and Databases

Spreadsheets — The Basics 33
Spreadsheets — Simple Formulas 34
Spreadsheets — Graphs and Charts 35
Spreadsheet Models and Simulations 36
Databases 37
Revision Summary for Section Five 38

Section 6 — The Internet

Internet Basics 39
Researching a Topic 40
Searching for Information 41
Fact and Opinion 43
Design a Web Page 44
Creating a Web Page 45
Creating a Web Page — the Harder Bits 46
Design a Website 47
E-mail 48
Address Books 49
Revision Summary for Section Six 50

Section 7 — Computers in the Real World

Computers in Shops 51
More Computer Applications 52
Even More Computer Applications 53
Measurement — Data Logging 54
Logging Period and Logging Interval 55
Measuring Physical Data 56
Computers and the Law 57
Computers and the Workplace 58
Computer Use — Health and Safety Issues 59
Revision Summary for Section Seven 60

Published by Coordination Group Publications Ltd.

Contributors:

Charley Darbishire
Colin Harber Stuart
Kerry Kolbe
Simon Little
Andy Park
Glenn Rogers
Claire Thompson

ISBN:1-84146-291-8
Groovy website: www.cgpbooks.co.uk
Jolly bits of clipart from CorelDRAW
Printed by Elanders Hindson, Newcastle upon Tyne.
Text, design, layout and original illustrations
© Coordination Group Publications Ltd 2002
All rights reserved.

Data

Right, no messing about then — a computer is simply a machine that processes data. And this being ICT, you have to make sure you know <u>what data is</u> and what a computer does with it.

Data has No Meaning

Data is <u>information</u> that has <u>no meaning</u>.

Suppose someone walks up to you and gives you a piece of paper with 120987 written on it. The number could mean <u>absolutely anything</u>. They might be telling you their birthday, or how much money you owe them, or they might be giving you their phone number (if you're lucky).

Data only becomes information when you know the <u>context</u> of the data.

...which means that x multiplied by the sum of the hairs in my nose squared is proportional to...

Example of data

Information = Data + Meaning

1) <u>Computers</u> are machines that <u>process data</u>. They're <u>stupid</u> — they don't understand the data they process.

2) If you get a computer to process data that's incorrect, the results will be meaningless. This is called <u>Garbage In, Garbage Out (GIGO)</u>.

3) Some people call this 'computer error'. They're wrong — it's human error. Computers hardly ever make mistakes. They just do what they're <u>programmed</u> to do.

If you program a computer to work out the total cost of buying fifty pizzas at £2.99 each, but you type in £29.9 by mistake, you'll get the <u>wrong answer</u>.

Data is stored in Bytes

Computers run on <u>electricity</u> — try using a computer without it. They're made up of a number of electric <u>circuits</u>, and each circuit can either be on or off.

Computers use a <u>binary code</u> (i.e. they use only 2 digits) to represent data. A circuit that's switched <u>on</u> represents the digit <u>1</u>, and a circuit that's switched <u>off</u> represents the digit <u>0</u>.

Morse code works in a similar way — it's either a dot or a dash.

Bit	Each individual 1 or 0 is called a <u>bit</u> — short for <u>binary digit</u>.
Byte	<u>8 bits</u> is called a <u>byte</u>.
Kilobyte	<u>1 kilobyte</u> (1 Kb, or simply 1 K) is about a <u>thousand</u> bytes.
Megabyte	<u>1 megabyte</u> (1 Mb) is about a <u>million</u> bytes.
Gigabyte	<u>1 gigabyte</u> (1 Gb) is about a <u>thousand million</u> bytes.

I store my food in bites too.

First page of this book — what a data remember...

Here's some rather useless information... 1 kilobyte = 2^{10} = 1024 bytes, and 1 megabyte = 2^{20} = 1 048 576 bytes, and even more interesting... 1 gigabyte = 2^{30} = 1 073 741 824 bytes.

Computer Systems

ICT is <u>dead simple-ish</u> if you know about the <u>three parts of a computer system</u>...

(A) Data is Entered at the Input Stage

1) Information is <u>converted</u> into data before it's <u>entered</u> into the computer.

2) This might mean having to convert information into a <u>code</u>.

3) For example the date <u>26th September 1964</u> might be converted into <u>260964</u>.

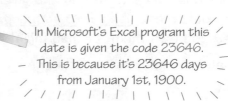

In Microsoft's Excel program this date is given the code 23646. This is because it's 23646 days from January 1st, 1900.

4) The data that's been entered should be <u>validated</u> (checked) to make sure it's of the <u>right type</u> (e.g. a percentage should be between 0 and 100).

5) The data should also be <u>verified</u> — in other words it should be <u>correct</u> (e.g. if the examination mark was 67% then 67 should have been entered).

(B) The Computer then Processes the Data

Ah... a day in the sun. That dodgy sick note turned a school day into a holiday... It worked a treat.

1) <u>Processing</u> involves turning the input data into <u>something else</u>.

2) For example a set of examination results could be put into a computer which then <u>calculates</u> the average score.

> Processing is carried out using the computer's Central Processing Unit (CPU).

(C) The Results are then Shown at the Output Stage

1) Output is when the computer communicates the <u>results</u> of the data processing to the user.

2) The two most common ways are a <u>screen display</u> and <u>print out</u>.

3) At this point the data becomes information again.

4) The information obtained at the output stage might then be used as <u>feedback</u> to <u>input more data</u>. This turns the system into a <u>cycle</u> (also know as a <u>feedback loop</u>).

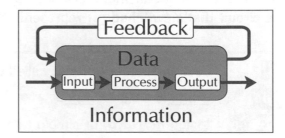

> Remember: input, processing and output

Input at 4, processed at school & work for 60 years, then output onto a couch...

Input, processing, and then output... that's all computers are. Make sure you remember that. Don't spend all your time in ICT lessons texting your mates about what you're going to do tonight.

Computerised vs. Manual Systems

Let's face it — computers are pretty expensive. Well, more expensive than a lot of things anyway. So there's <u>no point</u> buying an expensive computer system unless it's going to be <u>worth the money</u>.

Using a Computer System has lots of Benefits...

The government stores information about all the cars registered in the UK on a large <u>computer database</u>. It could also store the same information in a <u>manual paper-based system</u>. There are <u>six main advantages</u> to using a <u>computerised system</u>:

> **BENEFITS** of a <u>computerised</u> system:
>
> 1) Takes up <u>a lot less space</u> — no need for grey filing cabinets.
>
> 2) <u>Searching</u> for records is <u>very quick</u>.
>
> 3) <u>More than one person</u> at a time can access the same data from their network PC.
>
> 4) The data stays <u>within</u> the computer's <u>memory</u> — it <u>won't get lost or misfiled</u>.
>
> 5) <u>Fewer staff</u> are needed to look after the computer system.
>
> 6) <u>Reports</u> can be <u>generated</u> very <u>quickly</u>. In a paper-based system, reports can only be written after looking at each relevant record and transferring information <u>by hand</u>. This is <u>time-consuming</u> and there's a chance of <u>human error</u>.

...but there are Plenty of Problems as well

There are <u>four main problems</u>:

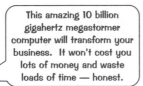

This amazing 10 billion gigahertz megastormer computer will transform your business. It won't cost you lots of money and waste loads of time — honest.

① <u>Setting up</u> a computer system is very <u>expensive</u>. <u>Big systems</u> in large organisations such as the **NHS** can <u>cost millions</u> of pounds.

② Computer systems <u>need people</u> to maintain and use them. <u>Training costs</u> can be high — and the money is <u>wasted</u> if the person leaves.

③ Computer systems are <u>not perfect</u> — if there's a <u>system failure</u> or a <u>power cut</u>, then important data might get <u>corrupted</u> or <u>lost</u>.

④ It can be <u>easy to copy files</u> and so remove confidential information from the system. The system needs to be <u>kept secure</u> from <u>unauthorised users</u> and <u>hackers</u>.

> Most people think that the benefits outweigh the problems — just about every organisation today uses computers.

See that bloke up there... that's your best mate, that is...

What's that bloke doing on this page here... trying to sell me dodgy computer systems... with a million and one shining teeth like some rabid dog. There was a white space and then there he was.

Network Security

There are three main types of network security: <u>access</u> security, <u>data</u> security and <u>physical</u> security.

Access Security Limits a Person's Use of the Network

1) All <u>authorised users</u> should be given <u>user names</u> and create their own <u>passwords</u>. This will limit <u>unauthorised access</u> to the network.

2) Users should <u>change</u> their password <u>frequently</u>.

3) Individual users can be assigned <u>access rights</u> — for example network managers can be given access to the software that controls how the network is run. Other users can be <u>limited</u> to <u>certain types</u> of <u>applications software</u> such as word processors.

Data Security Prevents Loss of Data

1) Some software and files can be <u>password-protected</u> so that a password is needed to <u>view and amend</u> data.

2) Files can be made <u>read-only</u>, so that they cannot be altered or deleted. Other files may be <u>hidden</u> so that they're not visible to the user.

3) Regular <u>back-ups</u> should be made of the data on the system using suitable <u>backing storage</u>.

4) <u>Back-up files</u> should be kept secure — ideally in <u>locked fireproof rooms</u> in a <u>different location</u> to the network.

5) <u>Archiving</u> means copying or moving a file somewhere for <u>long-term</u> storage.

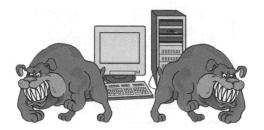

Physical Security Protects the Hardware

 Protect hardware with the 7 <u>SAD FLAB</u> rules.

Hardware is <u>expensive</u> — follow these 7 <u>SAD FLAB</u> rules to keep it safe:

1) `Serial numbers` — Keep a record of all <u>serial numbers</u>, and mark the organisation's name and postcode on all equipment — this helps police to identify stolen property.

2) `Alarms` — Computer rooms should be protected by <u>burglar alarms</u>.

3) `Doors` should be locked when the rooms are not in use.

4) `Fire protection` — Use fireproof doors and smoke alarms. Also, automatic <u>gas-flooding systems</u> could be used to put out any fire to prevent water damaging the equipment.

5) `Lock` windows to prevent access.

6) `Avoid` putting computers on the ground floor of buildings, where they can be easily seen from outside.

7) `Blinds` or curtains should be closed at night, and monitors should be switched off, so the computers are less visible.

They're all out to get me... all of them I tell you... out to get me...

Lock your doors and windows, close your blinds, password-protect your computer, hire a multi-million pound security force... You don't want your parents to know what you look at on the net.

Input Devices

An input device is any <u>hardware</u> which is used to <u>enter data</u> into the computer system.

QWERTY Keyboards are the Most Common Input Device

1) QWERTY keyboards are the most common type of keyboards. The name comes from the <u>first row of letters</u> on the keyboard.

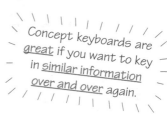

2) QWERTY keyboards are based on the design of the first typewriters.

3) A problem is that keying in can be slow unless the user has been <u>trained</u> or knows how to type.

Concept Keyboards are Faster but More Limited

1) Concept keyboards are often found in <u>shops</u> and <u>restaurants</u>. Each key has a <u>symbol</u> (or word) on it, representing a piece of data (e.g. the <u>price</u>) stored in the computer.

2) For example, if you go to a fast-food restaurant and order a bacon-triple-lard burger, the assistant will press the picture of that burger. The CPU then tells a <u>display panel</u> to show the correct price and sends a message to the kitchen and stock-control.

Concept keyboards are <u>great</u> if you want to key in <u>similar information</u> <u>over and over</u> again.

Mouses and the like...

Most people find using a mouse <u>easy</u>. A mouse has <u>two main parts</u>:

1) The <u>buttons</u>. When the cursor is over an icon, menu item, or the edge of a picture, the mouse buttons can be <u>clicked</u> or <u>double-clicked</u>. The button can also be <u>held down</u> to <u>drag</u> something across the screen.

2) Under the mouse is a <u>ball</u>. <u>Sensors</u> measure the movement of the ball in two directions. From this, the computer can work out the <u>direction and distance</u> the mouse has travelled. This is used to move the <u>cursor</u> on the <u>screen</u>.

<u>Laptops</u> have <u>tracker balls</u>, or little <u>pimples</u>, or touchy-feely <u>pads</u>:

1) A <u>tracker ball</u> works in the same way as a mouse, but the ball's moved <u>directly by the hand</u>, so it takes up less space. Most people find using them a bit <u>fiddly</u>, and not that accurate or quick.

2) <u>Touch-sensitive pads</u> look like <u>small screens</u>. You move your <u>finger</u> across the pad to move the <u>cursor</u>. They use <u>less space</u> than a mouse, but they're <u>easily damaged</u> and not very reliable.

3) <u>Little pimples</u> work by you putting a finger on them and pushing in some direction, which moves the cursor. They're really really small, not very accurate, and a bit weird.

Graphics Pads make Drawing Easier and More Accurate

1) Graphics tablets are like a pen and paper. They're made of a <u>touch-sensitive membrane</u> (like the piece of paper) and a <u>rigid stylus</u> (like the pen).

2) The user presses on the surface with the stylus, and the membrane registers its <u>position</u>, and displays it on the <u>screen</u>.

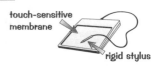
touch-sensitive membrane

rigid stylus

Mmmmm... look at that cheese... Mmmmm... Cheese...

Yes, yes... I know you already know what a mouse is, and what a keyboard is. But I've still got to stick it in just so I can say that this book covers everything you need to know. Fantastic...

Input Devices

Here are some input devices for you to get excited about. Make <u>sure</u> you know how they work.

Scanners Convert Images into Digital Data

1) A scanner works a bit like a <u>fax machine</u>. A picture is passed through the scanner and is <u>converted</u> into digital data.

2) <u>Problems</u> — these <u>bitmap files</u> can be very large and so take up a lot of <u>memory</u>.
<u>Benefits</u> — the scanned image can be <u>manipulated</u> and <u>edited</u> easily and quickly.

> *Small scanners are usually <u>hand-held</u>. Larger <u>flat-bed</u> scanners fit onto a worktop.*

Digital Cameras are a bit like Scanners

<u>Digital cameras</u> save an image as a series of dots called <u>pixels</u>. The image can then be <u>uploaded</u> to a computer and edited using <u>photo-editing software</u>.
<u>Benefits</u> — photographic <u>film is not needed</u> and the image is available for <u>immediate use</u>. It can also be sent as an <u>e-mail attachment</u> to anywhere in the world.
<u>Problem</u> — <u>high-resolution</u> images use <u>lots of memory</u> and currently use a <u>lot of battery power</u>.

Light Pens and Laser Scanners are used Loads

<u>Light pens</u> and <u>Laser scanners</u> are used in supermarkets and libraries. They are used to read a <u>bar code</u> which contains <u>data</u> about the <u>product</u> being <u>scanned</u>.
<u>Benefits</u> — it makes buying goods <u>faster</u> and <u>reduces</u> the chance of <u>human error</u>.
<u>Problems</u> — the system is <u>expensive</u> and depends on the data in the bar code and the computer system being <u>accurate</u>.

My favourite input device is a spoon.

Microphones convert Sound into Data

<u>Microphones</u> are used to input data into <u>voice-recognition systems</u>, which <u>convert sound</u> into <u>text or commands</u> for the computer. They are also used to <u>record sound</u> so it can be stored <u>digitally</u> and sent over the Internet or by e-mail.

Sensors change Environmental Information into data

<u>Sensors</u> are hardware that <u>record environmental information</u> and <u>convert</u> it to <u>data</u>. Examples include <u>temperature</u> sensors, <u>light</u> sensors and <u>infra-red</u> sensors used in burglar alarm systems.

Credit Cards have a Magnetic Stripe on the Back

(Unsurprisingly called <u>Magnetic Stripe Cards</u>.)

magnetic stripe

1) Magnetic stripe cards — made by sealing a short length of <u>magnetic tape</u> into the surface of a plastic card.
2) <u>Carry information</u> so the computer can identify the customer (credit/debit cards) or the number of units available (phone cards).

My camera thinks everything's groovy — it's a dig-it-all camera...

Wow. Look at all these things you should know about. Credit cards, and sensors, and microphones, and digital cameras, and scanners, and light pens and lasers and that's filled this box.

Revision Summary for Section One

Oh, oh, Section One's not quite over yet. You've read up on the basic bits and bobs — have a quick go at these questions and see how much of this you've got into your head. Scribble down your answers then check back through the section. Think you've cracked it? Roll right along to Section Two. If you get any wrong, nip back to those bits for another look. Then throw the book down and get doing something fun instead...

1) Explain the difference between data and information.

2) In what way are computers stupid?

3) What do the letters GIGO stand for?

4) How many bits are there in a byte?

5) What are the three stages in the processing of data called?

6) What happens at each stage?

7) Give four reasons why a computerised information system is better than a paper-based one.

8) Explain two problems with using a computerised system.

9) Who should have the right to know your password?
   a) You
   b) Your best mate
   c) Anyone who might want to delete your files

10) What does 'read-only' mean?

11) What does 'archiving' mean?

12) Describe three things you can do to help keep your hardware safe.

13) Where should back-up files be stored?
   a) In a cardboard box under your desk
   b) A secure place in a different building
   c) In Preston

14) What are the first six letters on a normal keyboard?

15) How are concept keyboards different to normal keyboards?

16) Describe how a mouse works.

17) Explain one difference between a touch-sensitive pad and a mouse.

18) What would you use a rigid stylus for?
   a) Writing on a graphic tablet
   b) Unscrewing the casing of your computer
   c) Picking your nose

19) What type of file is created when an image is put through a scanner? Why is it called this?

20) Describe two benefits of using a laser pen or light scanner system.

21) Explain two problems with using them.

22) What do sensors do? Give examples of two types of sensor.

23) What do you call a donkey with three legs?

Data Capture

Data capture is gathering information to put on a computer system.

Data Capture turns Information into Data

Data capture (or collection) is a two-part process:

1) You have to record the information in a suitable form for the computer.
2) You have to actually enter the data onto the computer.

Manual Methods — Forms and Questionnaires

Manual methods include data-capture forms and questionnaires. Someone writes down information in a preset way (e.g. on a form). It's then input into the computer exactly as it was written on the form.

1) Questionnaires usually need someone to key in the results by hand.

2) But with some data-capture forms you just enter information in code format. The information is automatically read using a scanner-type thing. E.g. computerised school registers, multiple-choice answer sheets...

> 21. You are driving along the motorway and you hit a rabbit. Do you:
>
> A: Stop and walk back to pick it up.
> B: Continue driving.
> C: Pull onto the hard shoulder and ring the vet.
> D: Drive over it a few times, just to make sure.
>
> A B C D
> ☐ ☐ ☐ ☐

3) Turnaround documents (e.g. electricity-meter-reading forms) use a semi-automatic system. The computer system prints a personalised form, with a space to record the meter reading. The customer writes on the reading by hand, then the electricity company adds the new data to the customer record on the computer.

Automatic Methods — Sensors and that...

1) Automatic data capture means collecting information from sensors, bar-code readers and scanners.

2) For example, a temperature sensor records the temperature, and stores this data until it's downloaded onto a computer for processing.

Each Method has its Advantages

MANUAL DATA-CAPTURE SYSTEMS

1. Sometimes necessary — information such as personal details can only be obtained using a manual data-capture form.
2. Cheaper — less hardware and software needed, so the system will be less expensive.

AUTOMATIC DATA-CAPTURE SYSTEMS

1. Faster and more accurate than manual systems.
2. Humans don't have to be present — so it's useful in dangerous or inaccessible places (e.g. nuclear reactors).

Manual, automatic — well, any car would be nice...

Learn the difference between manual and automatic data capture — and an example or two of each. Then go through the advantages and disadvantages of each. If you've really learnt it all, you'll be able to close this book and write it all down on a bit of paper. Try it.

Data Capture — Form Design

It's important that data-capture forms are <u>well designed</u> — if the person filling the form in doesn't do it properly, the data will be useless.

Follow these Rules for a Well-Designed Form:

KEEP IT SIMPLE...

1) Keep the layout <u>simple</u>. Leave enough <u>space</u> to write answers, and don't put answer boxes <u>too close</u> together — or information can get put in the wrong box by mistake.

2) Write the instructions in <u>simple language</u>. Make it obvious what to do.

3) Make it <u>look</u> interesting. (Different <u>font styles</u> and <u>sizes</u> can help.)

KEEP IT USEFUL...

1) Don't ask for <u>too much</u> information. There's <u>no point</u> requesting information you've already got — or don't need.

2) If possible, get people to write information in a <u>suitable way</u> for entering as <u>data</u>. E.g. you could ask people to give their date of birth in the form <u>dd/mm/yyyy</u>.

KEEP IT ACCURATE...

1) <u>Check</u> the form thoroughly for <u>accuracy</u> and <u>completeness</u> before it is printed.

2) Most importantly — <u>TEST IT</u>. Try it out on a small sample of people to make sure it works OK. If anything's wrong, you can sort it out before you use it for real.

Examples:

This is a <u>badly designed</u> form. The layout is muddled and the instructions are very vague.

Vampires R Us — Customer Details Form

Vampires R Us PLC
The Old Caves
Bytingham
Cumbria

Please fill in this form and let us have it back.

Telephone number..........

Name and Address:
....
....
....

When would you like to get bitten?
....
....

This is <u>much better</u>...

VAMPIRES R US — CUSTOMER DETAILS FORM

VAMPIRES R US PLC, THE OLD CAVES, BYTINGHAM, CUMBRIA

Please write your details in the spaces below and return to the above address by October 31st 2003. Thank you.

First name: .... Last name: ....
Address Line 1: ....
Address Line 2: ....
Address Line 3: ....
Address Line 4: ....
Address Line 5: ....
Night time telephone number: ....
At what time of night would you like us to visit you? Please tick one box only.

bm	Before midnight	
m	At midnight	
am	After midnight	

Form? — I thought that was the stuff in my sorfa...*

You wouldn't really think there was that much to it, would you. Still, there you go. Remember — the most important thing is to test it. Then if you have drawn up a shoddy form, you'll find out before you get 500 shoddily filled-in forms back. You know it makes sense.

*You will only get this if you live north of Manchester.

Benefits and Problems of Data Collection

Once you've captured all this information, it has to be stored somewhere. Electronic storage is great, but there are problems. Sit back and enjoy *"When Good Data Collection Goes Bad"*...

Collected Data needs to be Protected

Bank Customers Hacked Off

Bank staff got it in the neck today as thousands of account holders had their entire savings wiped off the computer system.

Hackers got into bank records last night and changed thousands of account balances, meaning that shoppers today were unable to draw money from their accounts. Bank staff faced a deluge of complaints from disgruntled customers.

Spokesman Terry Jones said, "we are trying very hard to rectify the situation".

HACKERS

1. Hackers can sometimes "hack" into a computer system (hence the name) and look at files. Which isn't great for privacy.
2. They can also sometimes change or delete bits while they're at it.

DATA CAN BE LOST

Sometimes you just lose data — can't get at what you've stored — because of things like:

1. Hardware failure,
   e.g. faulty equipment, power cuts.
2. Physical damage to the computer,
   e.g. microwaving it, throwing it out of the window.

Spilled Tea Mayhem at WI

Foxton WI had a nasty shock this week when the treasurer's computer blew up — losing the whole season's fantasy football scores.
"I spilled my tea on the computer and it started to smoke, then 'bang!'" said Mrs Myrtle of Lowestoft Road. "They might be able to fix the computer, but they can't get back the football scores."

Sir Cam Wreaks Havoc

Over the last two weeks, the e-mail virus "Sir Cam" has swept through millions of computers. It is thought to be the most sophisticated e-mail virus ever.

Consultants say that smaller companies are often hit the worst — because their anti-virus protection isn't kept up to date.

VIRUSES

Everyone's heard of them but most people haven't a clue what they are.

1. A virus is a program that can make copies of itself and moves between computers by attaching itself to files and e-mails.
2. It can corrupt files — making them unusable.
3. This causes huge problems for many companies, who face losing vital customer or business data.

The Data Storage Debate — Computer or Paper?

So how come everyone uses computers then...
There are more details on this stuff on page 3, but here's a quick reminder:

ADVANTAGES OF USING COMPUTERS

1. Quick and easy to *search for records*.
2. Takes up *less space* than filing cabinets.
3. *Fewer staff* needed.
4. Easier to produce *reports* and *analyse data*.
5. *More than one person* can look at the data at the same time.

DISADVANTAGES OF USING COMPUTERS

1. *Expensive* to set up.
2. *Staff* need to be *trained* to use the system.
3. Data is *not completely safe* (see above).
4. *Confidential files* can be *read* or copied more easily than if they were locked in a filing cabinet.

Fire... flood... famine... computer viruses...

Learn the three main ways you can lose data if it's stored on computer (and how to prevent it). Then learn the pros and cons for businesses (etc.) of storing data on computer rather than paper.

Data Storage and Processing

Once you've captured your data, it gets stored and processed in certain ways.

Data Files are Organised into Fields and Records

Data files have to be organised in some way before they're stored.
They're usually organised in the form of records and fields, like this:

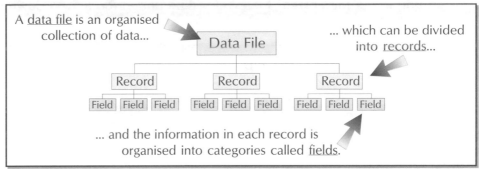

A <u>data file</u> is an organised collection of data... → Data File ... which can be divided into <u>records</u>...

Record   Record   Record

Field Field Field   Field Field Field   Field Field Field

... and the information in each record is organised into categories called <u>fields</u>.

Fields can be Fixed Length or Variable Length

The <u>length</u> of a field is the number of <u>characters</u> (i.e. numbers, letters or symbols) that it contains.
The longer the field, the more memory it uses.

FIXED-LENGTH FIELDS

1) Have a <u>fixed number of characters</u>.
2) The data file allows <u>exactly that number of characters</u> — whether they're needed or not.
3) Fixed-length fields are <u>quicker</u> to process but use <u>a lot of memory</u>.

VARIABLE-LENGTH FIELDS

1) A <u>variable-length</u> field is <u>only as long</u> as it <u>needs</u> to be.
2) E.g. a field containing 'Boris' takes up <u>5</u> characters, but one with '<u>Bob</u>' just <u>3</u>.
3) Variable-length fields use <u>less memory</u>, but <u>take longer</u> to process.

Real-time Processing and Batch Processing

There are a few different ways that computers can process data — the two most important ones are <u>real-time processing</u> (updates as you go) and <u>batch processing</u> (all in one "batch").

REAL-TIME PROCESSING

1) <u>Real-time</u> processing is when data files are updated <u>as soon as</u> new information is entered or becomes <u>available</u>.
2) E.g. when you <u>book a seat</u> on an aeroplane, it's booked straight away — so no one else can book the same seat.
3) Use real-time processing when you need to process the information straight away.

BATCH PROCESSING

1) <u>Batch</u> processing is when loads of jobs are <u>stored up</u>, and then all processed at once.
2) E.g. large businesses work out the <u>wages</u> for all their employees at the same time each month.
3) Use batch processing when you've got to process a <u>large volume</u> of data <u>regularly</u> — and where the processing doesn't have to be done immediately.

Let's see how much of this data you've stored then...

Eeesh — there's a lot to get your teeth into here. At the end of the day, there's just no substitute for sitting down and learning this stuff. Once you know it all inside out, you'll have no problems.

Data Presentation

It depends what <u>output devices</u> you've got, what data you've got, and how you want it to come across.

Information can be Presented in Six Different Ways...

1) <u>TEXT</u> is best used when you need to communicate ideas <u>precisely</u>. With properly written text, both writer and reader understand the words — so you know the correct meaning will be understood. The down side is that <u>difficult</u> ideas often need <u>a lot of words</u> to explain them.

WE HAVE JUST HIT AN ICEBERG AND WILL BE SINKING IN APPROXIMATELY 30 MINUTES. PLEASE DO NOT PANIC.

2) <u>SOUND</u> can be used not only to communicate words — but also to add music or sounds to give the listener a sense of place or mood. You don't have to view a screen to receive the message, but you do need a <u>sound card</u> and <u>speakers</u> (or headphones) to hear it.

3) <u>PICTURES</u> (either still or moving) can also communicate ideas and emotions better than words. However, the message can be <u>ambiguous</u> — people can interpret pictures in different ways.

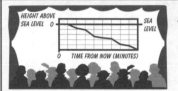

4) <u>GRAPHS</u> show the <u>relationship</u> between two or more sets of numbers using lines, dots and bars plotted between axes, e.g. <u>line graphs</u> and <u>bar graphs</u>. Graphs can accurately <u>summarise</u> complex information, but the reader needs some mathematical skill to read them.

5) <u>CHARTS</u> are any image that communicates <u>numerical</u> or <u>logical</u> information, e.g. <u>tables</u>, <u>pie charts</u> and <u>flow charts</u>. (They have the same pros and cons as graphs.)

Number of people who will die when this ship sinks — Won't die: 5% — Will die: 95%

When Your Ship Sinks — Click here for a video of a ship sinking — VIDEO — Click here for full details of the impending disaster — INFO — Click here for free safety advice — HELP — Click here for that annoying Celine Dion song to put you in the mood — MUSIC

6) <u>MULTIMEDIA PRESENTATIONS</u> combine text, graphics and sound, like in a CD-ROM encyclopaedia.

... Using Two Main Output Methods

1) <u>SCREEN DISPLAY</u> is the most common method. The user simply views the information on their <u>VDU</u> or <u>monitor</u> (and also hears any sounds played through a <u>loudspeaker</u>).

2) <u>HARD COPY</u> is a permanent <u>printed</u> record of the information — usually on <u>paper</u>.

Each Method has Pros and Cons

1) With <u>screen displays</u>, information can be seen or edited <u>immediately</u>, and multimedia presentations using <u>sound</u> and <u>moving images</u> are possible.

2) What you see on screen might not look exactly the same as the final printed version.

3) <u>Hard copies</u> are good because they give a <u>permanent</u> record of the information, and can be viewed <u>without a computer</u>. On the other hand, you can't use sounds and moving images.

... or you could just get CGP to write a book on it...

Oi. No nodding off at the back. I'm working my fingers to the bone here to make this stuff as interesting as I possibly can. <Ahem> Right. Good. Remember — there are loads of different ways to present information oh god this stuff's dull I give up you can go back to sleep if you like...

Revision Summary for Section Two

Ah... Section Two — What a beauty. Everything from fields to mice. No fieldmice though. Still, you can't have everything. OK, on with the show — test your knowledge with these searching questions... and don't stop 'til you've got the lot.

1) What are the two parts to data capture?

2) Give an example of each of these methods of data capture:
   a)   manual methods
   b)   semi-automatic methods
   c)   automatic methods

3) Give two advantages each of manual and automatic data capture systems.

4) How should instructions be written on a data capture form?
   a)   Using complex syntax and vocabulary to communicate elementary linguistic structures,
   b)   In plain English,
   c)   In binary.

5) List four other things to remember when designing a data capture form.

6) List as many examples as you can of ways your stored data can be lost (make it at least three, or I'll know you're not trying).

7) Write down one advantage and one disadvantage of storing data on a computer as opposed to paper.

8) How are data files organised?
   a)   In fields and records
   b)   In fields of wheat
   c)   In filing cabinets

9) What's the difference between fixed-length fields and variable-length fields?

10) Describe real-time processing. Give one example of where it might be used.

11) Do the same for batch processsing.

12) List four different ways you can present information.

13) What's the downside of using a hard copy instead of a screen display for a presentation?

14) What's the difference between a graph and a chart?

15) What comes after Section Two?

Step One — Identify the Problem

This is probably the scariest bit of ICT. Systems analysis is the way that <u>old information systems</u> <u>are turned into new improved ones</u>. Your hilarious teacher will probably think it's really cool to get you to pretend you're a systems analyst and solve a problem using ICT. It may not be, but just play along, okay.

The System Life Cycle shows how Changes are Implemented

This diagram is dead useful — it helps you to see how all the bits in this section fit together.

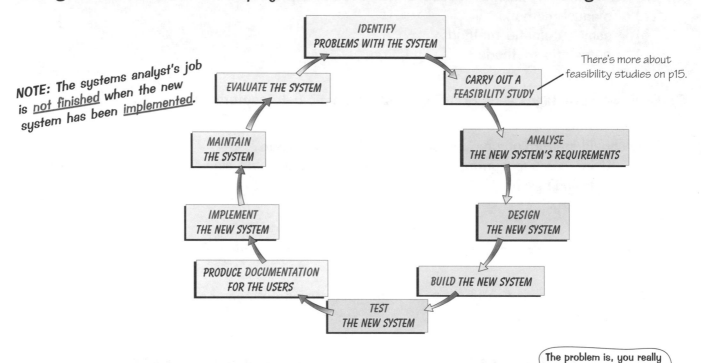

NOTE: The systems analyst's job is <u>not finished</u> when the new system has been <u>implemented</u>.

There's more about feasibility studies on p15.

How to Identify the Problem...

1) There are <u>two main problems</u> with existing systems:
   - there might be a <u>manual system</u> where a computerised system would be better,
   - or there might be problems because the <u>existing computer</u> system isn't good enough.

2) The systems analyst needs to:
   <u>interview</u> users of the system to find out their experiences,
   <u>analyse</u> the results of questionnaires given to the users,
   <u>observe</u> people using the system,
   <u>study</u> documents such as user guides, printouts and error reports.

3) The systems analyst should then <u>understand</u> the present system and its <u>problems</u>.

4) This information is then used to help <u>analyse the new system</u> and produce the <u>feasibility study</u>.

The problem is, you really need to be using a mouse.

A system analyst's work is never done...

You need to <u>learn the System Life Cycle</u> — properly.
It's no fun at all, but it's the only way any of this stuff is going to make <u>any kind of sense</u>.
Start by learning the words in <u>red</u> — they should help jog your memory for the rest of it.

Analysis — The Feasibility Study

A <u>feasibility study</u> is where you analyse the <u>requirements</u> of the new system — to <u>help you decide</u> whether it's <u>worth doing</u>. You need to do each of these things in order, then go back to the start.

① Decide on the Objectives for the New System

<u>Objectives</u> are measurable <u>outcomes</u> that can <u>test</u> whether it's an <u>improvement</u> or not.
You need <u>a few</u> of them to be sure.

E.g. "to <u>reduce</u> the <u>time</u> needed to <u>print the wage slips</u> by <u>25%</u>"

This is a <u>good</u> objective because you can test it by <u>measuring</u> and then <u>comparing</u> the time taken on the old and new systems.

② List the Inputs and Outputs for the New System

<u>INPUTS</u> — any <u>data</u> that's going <u>into</u> the system

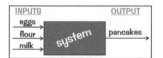 **Examples** *prices of goods, customer orders, new customer details, details of returned goods, employee details, salary details, employee hours...*

<u>OUTPUTS</u> — any <u>documents</u>, etc coming <u>out of</u> the system

invoices, internal reports, statistics, price tags, wage slips, personalised employee timesheets or letters, etc.

INPUTS eggs flour milk → **system** → **OUTPUT** pancakes

③ Write Down the Rules and Constraints of the System

The <u>rules</u> of the system are how various <u>factors</u> or constraints <u>affect the operation</u>.
That's things like:

"if there's a sudden trend for a product, we might sell out"
"if the price of potatoes goes up, we'll have to charge more for chips"
"if we charge more for chips, not as many people will buy them"

Here are some more examples of <u>constraints</u> that affect how the business can operate:

Bob's business had more constraints than most...

TYPE OF CONSTRAINT	EXAMPLES
Space	... Size of shop/warehouse/office will limit number of different products stocked, numbers of staff, types of machinery used, etc.
Money (the most obvious one, I guess)	... restricts how fancy a computer system you can get, how many staff you can employ, the level of stocks you can buy, etc. Etc. etc.
Supply and Demand	... you have to stock what people want to buy, and you can't sell stuff if you can't get hold of it in the first place
Health and Safety	... can restrict the layout of the office/shop/warehouse, types of machinery used, methods of food preparation, etc. (the list is endless — ask any employer about health and safety and watch them wince...)
Shelf-Life	Some products can only be kept for a certain length of time, so you shouldn't buy more than you can sell before the sell-by date. Or you may have to destroy stock or risk being sued for selling out-of-date stuff.
Timing	If there's a sudden huge demand for a certain product, you may not be able to get the stock in time to satisfy the order, etc.

Use these <u>rules</u> to draw up a <u>model of the system</u> to show <u>how it works</u>.
<u>Go back</u> to your <u>objectives</u> to check the <u>new system</u> is an <u>improvement</u>.

All these rules and constraints — sounds like school...

I don't know about you, but I reckon this stuff all just looks <u>a bit random</u> to start off with.
But it does start to <u>make sense</u> once you've got <u>concrete examples</u> to work with, so stick with it.

Design — Input, Process, Output

This is the stage when the systems analyst really gets down to business. Make sure you know <u>what questions need to be asked</u> by the analyst — and how the <u>whole system fits together</u>.

Input — How the Data is Captured

1) The <u>input data</u> might need to be <u>organised</u> into fields of fixed or variable length.

2) The use of <u>codes</u> can <u>reduce</u> the <u>file size</u>.
   (*E.g. <u>gender</u> can be entered as <u>M or F</u> — reducing the number of <u>bytes</u> needed to <u>store</u> the data.*)

3) <u>Screen forms</u> should be sketched showing what the <u>user</u> will <u>see</u> whilst they input the data.

Input Checklist

Decide where the data will come from.	☐
Design the data-capture forms.	☐
Decide how the data needs to be structured.	☐
Decide how the data will be input.	☐
Design the input screen.	☐
Decide how the data will be validated.	☐

Process — What Happens to It

Process Checklist

List the tasks that need to be done.	☐
Write the commands that enable them to be done.	☐
Produce a plan to test if the processing works.	☐

1) The <u>tasks</u> that the system needs to perform should be based on the <u>original problem</u> and <u>objectives</u>.

2) The <u>commands</u> could include spreadsheet <u>formulas</u>, database <u>searches</u>, desktop publishing <u>page design</u>, and word-processing <u>mail-merge routines</u>.

3) The commands could also include <u>exchanging data</u> between <u>different applications</u>. (*E.g. <u>importing</u> a spreadsheet and using it to create a table in a word-processing package.*)

4) A <u>test plan</u> for the field '<u>month of birth</u>' might include <u>typical data</u> such as <u>6</u>, <u>extreme data</u> such as <u>12</u> and <u>invalid data</u> such as <u>Boris</u>. This will test whether the <u>data validation</u> works.

Output — Let it Out

1) The <u>Golden Rule</u> is to be <u>user-friendly</u>. This means that the output must be <u>appropriate</u> for the <u>needs of the audience</u>.

2) Users should only be <u>shown</u> the information that they <u>need</u> — and in a way they will easily <u>understand</u>.

3) <u>Layout</u> is as important as <u>content</u>.

4) The <u>layout</u> of <u>output screens</u> and <u>printouts</u> should first be <u>sketched</u> in rough and <u>shown</u> to the <u>user</u> to <u>check</u> they're <u>OK</u>.

Output Checklist

Decide which data needs to be output.	☐
Decide how to present the information.	☐
Decide which output devices to use.	☐
Design output screens.	☐

Input... output — shake it all about...

There are three big areas the systems analyst (that's you) needs to think about.
Learn these checklists for each bit, and the whole thing will be much clearer. OK, it probably won't suddenly become a doddle, but knowing what you need to think about is a good place to start.

Design — Flow Diagrams

Flow diagrams are great for working out the best order to do things. Here are a couple of different types — top-down diagrams and system flow charts. They're both pretty useful so get stuck in.

Top-Down Diagrams Set Out the Main Tasks

... and they look like this:

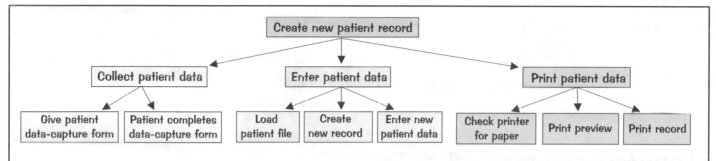

1) Top-down design looks at the whole system by breaking down the main tasks into smaller tasks.

2) Top-down diagrams show what has to happen — but not always how those things will happen.

System Flow Charts Show Exactly How the Data Moves

System flow charts use standard symbols — I've listed them down the side:
(The colours aren't standard, they're just to make it easier to follow... and they look nice.)

1) Here's a system flow chart for creating a new patient record at a surgery.

2) The patient fills in a data-capture form. The receptionist enters the information onto the patient record file.

3) If the data is invalid, it is checked against the actual form.

4) If the information has been input wrong, the receptionist needs to re-enter it.

5) If the information matches the original form, it goes back to the patient to check the details.

6) The new patient record is then used to create a mail-merged welcome letter.

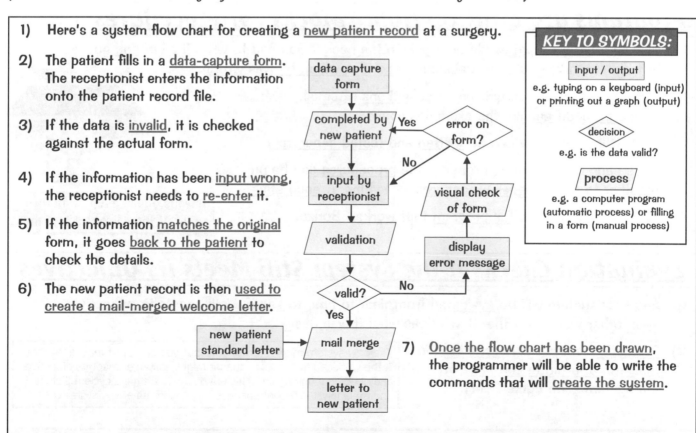

7) Once the flow chart has been drawn, the programmer will be able to write the commands that will create the system.

Flow diagrams — everyone's favourite topic for sure...

Top-down for breaking up the main tasks — system flow chart for the whole process in order.

Writing a Procedure

Most computer programs are made up of loads of <u>separate procedures</u>. Each procedure is written and tested separately, then the whole lot is put together to make the <u>entire program</u>.

Cause and Effect — Automated Ticket Barriers and That

You can write procedures where a <u>certain input</u> can <u>cause</u> a series of events to happen.
It's the good old input-process-output system again (see P.16).

EXAMPLES:

> Some traffic lights remain on "stop" until a car approaches: when this car drives onto the pressure pad (input), the traffic lights change (output).

> In car parks with ticket barriers: when you take the ticket (input), the barrier lifts up (output) to let the car in.

Counters can be used as Controls

Sometimes the <u>inputs</u> can be <u>linked to counters</u>, which will in turn act as <u>another input</u> that triggers <u>another output</u> when a certain <u>number is reached</u>.

> In the car park ticket barrier example, the "taking the ticket" input could be linked to a counter as well as to the barrier control. When the car park is full, the counter will produce another input and trigger a "FULL" sign to light up at the car park entrance. Clever, huh.

Programs are Built Up from "Blocks" of Procedures

1) Writing a <u>big program</u> would be a <u>pain in the neck</u> if you had to write it all in <u>one go</u>. If it didn't work, you'd have absolutely <u>no idea which bit was wrong</u>.

2) Instead, programs are written as <u>collections</u> of small, <u>simple procedures</u>, like the examples above.

3) Each little procedure can be <u>written</u> and <u>tested separately</u>.

4) Once each bit is working properly, the <u>procedures</u> can be put <u>together</u> to make <u>bigger procedures</u> — testing at <u>each stage</u>.

5) Eventually you get a <u>full program</u> that <u>works</u>. Bonza.

> **Always check each bit before you put the whole lot together...**

Evaluation Checks if the System Still Meets its Objectives

1) Any new system will be <u>evaluated</u> from time to time to <u>see if it still meets its objectives</u> — in other words whether it still does what it was designed to do.

2) <u>Evaluation</u> is basically <u>repeating</u> the <u>research you did at the start</u> of the system's life cycle (P.14).

> The new system might start off OK, but you can't just leave it at that. If the workload increases further, it might no longer meet its objectives and need updating again. This brings the system life cycle full circle and the analyst is brought back to begin work on a new system.

Programming — well it's a dull job but it pays a lot...

Well I'm sure you're all expert programmers now... OK maybe not, but this is the <u>backbone</u> of how <u>programming</u> and <u>control systems</u> work. And let's face it, you've got to start somewhere.

Revision Summary for Section Three

Systems Analysis may not make you leap for joy, but it's dead, dead important for businesses.
As the business grows, its IT requirements grow, blah, blah, blah. Anyway, just do the questions.
You'll thank me one day. Well, you won't, but I can pretend.

1) What is your name? Sorry, only kidding. What comes between analysing and implementing a new computer system?

2) List <u>three</u> ways you can gather information about the performance of an old system.

3) Why do a feasibility study?
    a)   Dunno
    b)   To check whether a new system is worth implementing
    c)   For a laugh, like

4) Give an example of an objective for a new system (don't use the one on page 15 — that's cheating).

5) What are the <u>three</u> main things that a feasibility study consists of?

6) List <u>four</u> types of constraints that may effect how a business operates.

7) List <u>three</u> things that should be done when designing a system's input.

8) List <u>three</u> things that should be done when designing a system's processes.

9) List <u>three</u> things that should be done when designing a system's output.

10) Describe what a top-down diagram is to someone who doesn't know.

11) Draw a system flow chart for making an omelette.

12) What are most computer programs made of?
    a)   Loads of separate procedures
    b)   Loads of nonsense
    c)   Cheese

13) Describe how counters can be used in car parks to tell motorists when the car park is full.

14) Once a new system has been implemented, it's evaluated from time to time. Why?

Word Processing Basics

Things have changed a lot since the days of the typewriter. Thanks to word processors, just about anyone can create a professional looking document. These two pages cover some of the simple features that make word processing so special.

Highlight text you want to edit

You're never going to write something that's perfect first time. So you need to know the different ways to edit what you've written. For most changes, you need to highlight (select) the text first:

Highlighting text with the mouse:

1) Double click to select a word. ...orse, out came the cabbage.

2) Click and drag with the mouse to select exactly what you want. ...g, expanding into unexplored territor... ...ng pop and looked down in horror.

3) Triple click to select a whole paragraph. Just when I thought things couldn't get worse, she brought out the cabbage. I knew I would be sick soon. I could feel my stomach swelling, expanding into unexplored territory. Suddenly, I heard something pop and looked down in horror.

Highlighting text with the keyboard:

Hold down shift while you move the text cursor with the cursor keys.

Hold down ctrl as well to select a word at a time.

...d now he walks with a limp. The poor man ca...

There are four ways to Edit Text

1) **DELETE** text. Use the backspace key to delete one character at a time. To delete a chunk of text, highlight it and press the backspace key.

2) **INSERT** and **REPLACE** text.
   To insert text, just click the cursor where you want it and start typing.
   To replace words or chunks of text, highlight the text you want to replace and start typing.

3) **MOVE** text using cut and paste or by highlighting and dragging it.

4) **REPEAT** text using copy and paste.

I must not make inappropriate noises or smells in class.

I must not make inappropriate noises or smells in class.
I must not make inappropriate noises or smells in class.
I must not make inappropriate noises or smells in class.
I must not make inappropriate noises or smells in class.
I must not make inappropriate noises or smells in class.
I must not make inappropriate noises or smells in class.

Ace time-saving tip: Next time your teacher gives you 200 lines, do them on a word processor with copy and paste.

LEARN THESE SHORTCUTS, PAL

CUT — CTRL X
COPY — CTRL C
PASTE — CTRL V
UNDO — CTRL Z

Cut and paste and copy and paste work in all programs, not just word processors. You'll use them **all the time** so learn these **keyboard shortcuts** for them.

Oh, and I've tagged UNDO on the end too.

TRUE STORY ABOUT UNDO: I once had a mad friend called Lindsay with big curly blonde hair (a bit like a poodle...). Err anyway, one day she crashed her Mini into a tree. Luckily she was fine, but her first thought after seeing what she'd done was "Ctrl Z"!

Admit it, this page has been one of the highlights of your life...

Try everything mentioned on this page. And practise each thing until you've got the hang of it. You may think some are a bit fiddly, but you'll quickly get the hang of them and they'll save you **LOADS** of time in the long run.

Word Processing Basics

Once you've got the words right, there's lots you can do to <u>jazz up</u> the appearance.

Four ways to change the look of your text

1) `CHANGE THE FONT` Font is the fancy name for the style of the letters.
You need to choose one which matches the tone of the document you're producing.

FISH FINGER   Fish finger   *Fish Finger*   FISH FINGER   **Fish finger** ← I wouldn't recommend this one — it's vile. Urrghh.

2) `CHANGE THE TEXT SIZE` Emphasise <u>headings</u> and <u>subheadings</u> by making them <u>larger</u>.
A font size between 10 and 12 point is easy to read for most people (this text is in 12 pt).
But small children and people with reading difficulties might need a larger font size.

3) `HIGHLIGHT THE TEXT` to make it stand out. There are four ways to do this:
    (i) **bold type**,   (ii) *italics,*   (iii) <u>underlined</u>,   (iv) colour.

4) `BULLETS AND NUMBERING` can be added for <u>lists</u> and <u>key points</u>. The computer automatically
does the numbers or bullets each time you press enter until you tell it to stop.

Three ways you can position your text

1. `INDENTING` Use the <u>tab key</u> to <u>indent</u> a line of text. Or you can indent a <u>whole paragraphs</u> to
make them stand out.

2. `ALIGNING AND JUSTIFYING`

Text is usually left-aligned like this text here. Bla bla bla bla blab lab lablab bla bla. Bla bla bla bla bla bla bla bla.	This text is right-aligned. Right-aligned text is sometimes used for addresses at the top of letters.	This text is centre-aligned. Bla bla bla bla blabla blbalblbla. bla bla bla blblbla bla bla burp bla bla. a bla blblbla bla bla bla bla.	This text is justified which means that each full line is exactly same length. Bla bloo bloap bling bla blay.

3. `LINE SPACING` <u>Line spacing</u> adjusts how far apart the lines of text are. <u>Double-line spacing</u> is
↕   ↕
much easier to read than <u>single-line spacing</u> — but it uses up much more paper.

Use the formatting toolbar (Luke)...

All decent word processors have a <u>formatting toolbar</u> like this.
Almost all the formatting you'll need to do can be done from here.

COLOURS AND BORDERS

FONT   TEXT SIZE   TEXT HIGHLIGHTING — BOLD, ITALIC AND UNDERLINE

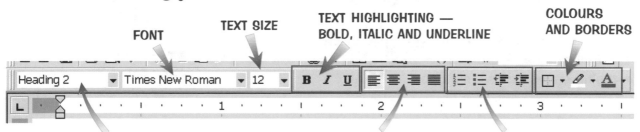

PARAGRAPH STYLES   ALIGNING AND TEXT JUSTIFICATION   BULLETS, NUMBERING AND INDENT.

The formatting toolbar will be with you always...

You need to become <u>intimately</u> acquainted with the formatting toolbar. He's your friend and will guide you up the steps to text-formatting <u>heaven</u>. A word of caution though, its very easy to get carried away and do things <u>because you can</u>, rather than because it's <u>helpful</u>. So always think what will be clear for your audience and keep things simple. T**h**at's MY A**D**v**ic**e anyway.

Word Processing — Advanced Features

On <u>tonight's menu</u>, we have tables, borders, columns, headers, footers and spell-checkers.

Tables, Borders and Columns can Help Readability

1) <u>Tables</u> are a good way to present <u>lists</u> of numerical or textual information, e.g. lists of names and addresses.

2) You can put <u>borders</u> around tables, pictures or blocks of text. This helps break up the information on the page — which sometimes makes it easier to read.

3) <u>Columns</u> can be created so that the text flows down the page and jumps automatically to the next column. This is great for newsletters and newspapers.

> ### Wordprocessing Weekly News
>
> Typists around the country were staggered to learn yesterday that text can be arranged automatically in columns.
>
> "I'm staggered," said 38-year-old Ian Denting. "If these newfangled word processors keep going at this rate then I'm going to become marginalised."
>
> Nelson Column, of London, said it had "absolutely nothing to do with me."

Headers and Footers are Good for Multi-Page Documents

Headers and footers are bits of information that go at the <u>top</u> and <u>bottom</u> of each page. They're usually things like the <u>date</u>, <u>filename</u>, <u>page number</u> ...

HEADER

FOOTER

Put headers into multi-page documents.

The good thing about them is the computer <u>automatically</u> puts the <u>correct one</u> on each page once you've told it what you want. This is particularly handy for things like page numbers.

Word processors can Check your Spelling

1) A <u>spell-checker</u> goes through your document and picks up any words that <u>aren't</u> in its <u>dictionary</u>.

Check you're smelling? Yep, I'm definitely smelling.

2) Spell-checkers generally find <u>two</u> types of error:
   - actual <u>misspelt</u> words   *e.g. fisialogical instead of physiological*
   - typing errors (known as typos)
     e.g. when you accidentally hit the wrong letter.

3) When the spell-checker finds a misspelt word, it tries to <u>guess</u> what you meant to type and gives you a list of <u>possible words</u>. It doesn't always guess right, but it's usually pretty good.

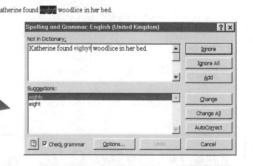

I HATE that paperclip, I HATE IT... why won't it GO AWAY...

Yes, there is one feature of a certain word processor I haven't mentioned. It can turn even the most mild-mannered person into a red raging rhinoceros. It's this fella here.

Aww, in't he cute...

Word Processing — Advanced Features

And for <u>dessert</u> we have templates, mail merge and importing information from other applications. You're already full? <u>Go on</u>, try a template... They're only <u>waffer-thin</u>.

Create Templates of Standard Documents

1) <u>Templates</u> are standard documents designed for a particular use. They save loads of time because the <u>layout</u> and <u>formatting</u> is already done — you just add the right text.

2) Word-processing packages come with a <u>range of templates</u> for different uses e.g. letters, memos, reports, CVs, newsletters, envelopes.

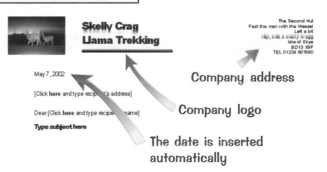

**Skelly Crag
Llama Trekking**

The Second Hut
Past the man with the Weasel
Left a bit
nip, nut a smelly drupp
Isle of Skye
BO13 X9P
TEL 01234 567890

May 7, 2002

[Click here and type recipient's address]

Dear [Click here and type recipient's name]

Type subject here

Company address

Company logo

The date is inserted automatically

Send out Personalised letters using Mail Merge

<u>Mail merge</u> lets you send personalised letters by combining a <u>standard letter</u> with information in a <u>database</u>. They save clubs and businesses loads of time — and there are three steps involved:

1) A <u>database</u> is created containing the information you want to appear in the personalised letter.

Andy uses mail merge to send love letters to all his girlfriends.

2) A <u>standard letter</u> is created containing codes, which are usually based on the field names in the database e.g. Dear <Surname> where 'Surname' is a field in the database.

3) The standard letter is linked to the database, and software <u>merges</u> the data by inserting each database record in turn into the letter. If there are 1000 names in the database then you'll get 1000 personalised letters — and each one will greet the reader by their <u>surname</u>.

Import Information from Other Applications

1) <u>Importing</u> means adding something created using a <u>different</u> software application. A good example is the use of <u>clip-art</u>.

2) When you <u>import</u> something, it becomes a separate <u>object</u> that you can move about and resize. But you <u>can't</u> edit it — you need to go back to the <u>original program</u> to do that.

I've stuck (<u>imported</u>) a graph from a <u>spreadsheet</u> program into my <u>word processor</u> document. I can move and resize it, but to change the graph, I need to open it from the spreadsheet program.

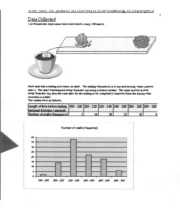

The bottom section of this page is really... .....(wait for it) ... IMPORTant

The best way to understand all these features is to go and <u>try them</u>. Then you'll realise they're not too hard at all. Mail-merge <u>sounds</u> really complicated but it's not, I promise. Go and have a play...

Graphics — Creating Images

You could draw <u>simple</u> images using a word processor.
But for <u>good-looking</u> graphics you need to use <u>graphics software</u>.

Images are Stored as either Bitmap or Vector Data

There are two types of graphics software.

Bitmap Buttercup

PAINTING SOFTWARE (<u>pixel-based</u> software)
1) Painting software is used for editing <u>bitmaps</u> — these are images made up of a series of coloured dots (<u>pixels</u>).
2) To edit the image, you basically alter each dot individually, although there are lots of different tools to make this easier.

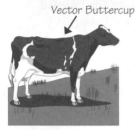
Vector Buttercup

DRAWING SOFTWARE (<u>vector-based</u> software)
1) Drawing software is used for creating and editing <u>vector graphics</u>. Each image is made up of separate lines and shapes (objects).
2) You change the image by editing these <u>objects</u>. You can stretch them, twist them, colour them and so on with a series of tools.

Vector graphics are <u>stored</u> differently to bitmaps which gives them much <u>smaller file sizes</u>.

Input Images using Scanners and Digital Cameras

There are two ways to put real images (e.g. photographs) onto the computer.

1) Use a <u>scanner</u>. You can scan in photographs, images from books or hand-drawings. The images are stored as <u>bitmaps</u> so the files can be very large (though they can be converted to other formats, e.g. JPEGs).

> A <u>JPEG</u> is a <u>compressed bitmap</u>. When you convert a bitmap to a JPEG, you <u>lose</u> some of the <u>picture quality</u>, but in a way that's <u>not noticeable</u> to the <u>human eye</u> — e.g. there might be slight colour changes. Compressing the image in this way can <u>massively reduce</u> the <u>file size</u>.

Resolution means the number of pixels (dots) making up the image.

300 dpi (dots per inch)   40 dpi (dots per inch)

The more pixels used, the sharper the image — but the bigger the file.

2) Use a <u>digital camera.</u> You then <u>download</u> the photos onto the computer. Digital photographs are initially stored as <u>JPEG</u> files — which are <u>usually</u> smaller than bitmaps, although the file size will depend on the level of resolution you've chosen.

Import Clip-Art images

1) <u>Clip-art images</u> are graphics and photos that have been created by someone else, but made available for you to use. Some come <u>free</u> with software packages, others can be <u>bought</u> on CD-ROM.

2) You can also copy images from the <u>Internet</u> but you have to be careful as a lot of them will be protected by <u>copyright</u>.

Beware of dodgy <u>80s clipart</u> like this. You could get a nasty shock if you're not expecting it.

Ah the 80s... Yazz, Yazoo, Prince, Kajagoogoo...great music... great hair...

Do you understand the difference between drawing and painting software? Are you sure?
Basically, with drawing software you use tools to <u>draw pictures</u> made up of separate objects.
CorelDraw and Adobe Illustrator are good drawing packages. With painting software, you start with a <u>bitmap image</u>, usually a photo, and use tools to alter an area of the picture or the whole thing (see p26). Good painting packages include Adobe Photoshop and Corel Photopaint.

Graphics — Changing Images

Graphics software is changing rapidly — especially <u>image manipulation</u> software for digital photos. But whatever the technology, the same basic <u>principles</u> still apply. Learn what they are.

Resize the Object — But try not to Distort it

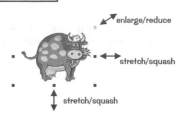
enlarge/reduce
stretch/squash
stretch/squash

1) Resizing a graphic is often done after the image has been <u>imported</u> into a word processor or desktop-publishing package.

2) It's usually done by selecting the graphic and then dragging one of the '<u>handles</u>' — outwards to make the image bigger, and inwards to make it smaller.

a bit stretched... oops

3) The clever bit is to keep the <u>proportions</u> of the image the <u>same</u> — in other words to keep it the same shape. Otherwise the image gets <u>distorted</u> and it can look pretty bad. In a lot of programs, you can do this by dragging the corner handle. You'd be amazed at how many publications contain distorted images.

Cropping Removes Unwanted Bits

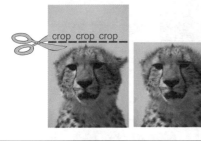
crop crop crop

1) <u>Cropping</u> removes parts of the image you don't want e.g. someone on the edge of the shot you want to get rid of.

2) It's a <u>quick</u> and <u>easy</u> way to remove bits of the image, although it can only remove whole <u>edges</u> — you can't use it to remove something in the <u>middle</u> of the graphic. Fortunately most graphics software has a separate tool to do this.

Rotate and Recolour Objects

Freda had yet another surreal dream involving rotated and recoloured images.

1) Images can be <u>rotated</u> to make them appear upside down, or <u>flipped</u> to appear back to front. Or you could make the Leaning Tower of Bradford by rotating an image just a little bit.

2) Images can also be <u>recoloured</u> — you can recolour the separate <u>objects</u> that make up a <u>vector</u> graphic. With <u>bitmap</u> images, you can use a <u>paint spray</u> or apply <u>colour effects</u> to the image (p.26).

Group Two or More Images Together

1) If you want to use an image that <u>isn't</u> in your clip-art library — for example a sheep riding a motorbike — but you <u>have</u> separate clip-art of a sheep and a motorbike, you can make a new object by <u>grouping</u> them together so that it looks like the sheep is riding the bike.

2) You can also select which graphics are at the <u>front</u> of the image and which are at the <u>back</u> — this is called <u>layering</u>.

This stuff CROPS up everywhere...

Get him off! Rubbish!

There are some <u>extremely powerful</u> graphics packages around now, which give you some really <u>flash</u> effects (if you've got a few days spare to teach yourself, that is). But if you're just making a poster for the school fête, you can probably <u>get away</u> with something a bit more <u>straightforward</u>.

Editing Digital Images

With painting programs like Adobe Photoshop and Corel Photopaint, you can <u>edit photos</u> in all sorts of <u>weird</u> and <u>wonderful</u> ways that you wouldn't have thought possible.

Adjust the Brightness, Contrast and Sharpness

Most of the time your photos won't need anything too fancy doing to them. But sometimes a scanned-in photo might be <u>too dark</u>, or a photo from a digital camera might look a bit <u>blurry</u>.

You can easily sort these out by adjusting the <u>brightness</u>, <u>contrast</u> and <u>sharpness</u>.

Filters let you produce Funky Effects

Any decent painting package will come equipped with a range of weird <u>filters</u> that let you change the <u>overall look</u> of the image. Here are just a few of them in action.

My pet caterpillar, JLo.

Original image   Distort filter   Plastic wrap filter   Stained Glass filter   Charcoal filter

Hue determines the colours

Altering the <u>Hue value</u> changes the <u>colours</u> used in the image. These groovy images of JLo were made simply by changing the Hue value.

Stick Parts of Images together to make Fake Photos

You can also use painting software to do some great <u>image-doctoring</u>.
It's quite fiddly at first, but with a bit of practice, you can create some great fake pictures.

Here's a photo I took of Britney the hippo driving my car. Ha ha fooled you... it's not real. I <u>created</u> it using Photoshop.

First, I drew round Britney with a <u>SELECTION TOOL</u> and created a <u>COPY</u> of that part of the image. Then I stuck Britney onto the image of my car.

Britney is on a different <u>LAYER</u> from the car, which means I can <u>move</u> and <u>resize her</u> without affecting the car image. The windscreen is also on a separate <u>transparent layer</u> in front of Britney.

Now you can create your own special photos of Britney...

I reckon I'm allowed to get overexcited on just one page in this book. So here we go...
Wow!!!! This stuff is <u>GREAT</u>!! No, really I mean it. It's just amazingly fantastically ace. Go and have a <u>play yourself</u> and then tell me you didn't LOVE it... Oh, I forgot to mention, you can also convert images to greyscale (black and white) which you need to do for things like newspapers and books.

Desktop Publishing — Basics

Most of the stuff I said about word processing is relevant to <u>desktop publishing</u> (<u>DTP</u>) as well. But there's a bit more to DTP...

DTP can create Professional Looking Pages

1) <u>Desktop publishing</u> software is used to build <u>professional</u> looking pages. It's the software used to produce all the newspapers, magazines and books that we read.

2) But you don't need to be an <u>expert</u> to use it — with a bit of practice, anyone can produce things like <u>posters</u>, <u>leaflets</u> and <u>newsletters</u>.

With DTP it's easy to create professional looking documents.

DTP Software is usually Frame-Based

1) Pages are built up as a series of <u>frames</u> — <u>text frames</u> containing text, <u>graphics frames</u> containing images and so on.

2) Frames can be <u>moved</u> or <u>resized</u>. This means that it is very easy to <u>edit</u> a DTP document by moving pictures or blocks of text around. Frames can also be moved from page to page.

3) DTP is a bit like making a <u>noticeboard</u> — you move about different bits of information until you're happy with the overall layout.

Each box-type thing is a frame.

Each picture or block of text forms its own frame that you can drag around separately.

Word processors <u>aren't</u> frame-based, so you can't move chunks of text or graphics without other stuff moving too.

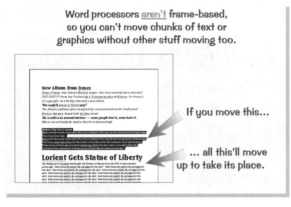

If you move this...

... all this'll move up to take its place.

4) DTP software usually lets the user create text and simple pictures — but it often works <u>best</u> when the source material is created in other <u>specialised</u> software (e.g. a word processor or a graphics package) and then <u>imported</u> into the DTP package.

DTP has Three Main Benefits

1) You can create very <u>professional-looking</u> documents — even with relatively <u>inexpensive</u> DTP packages. But the quality of the printed document is often limited by the quality of the <u>printer</u>.

2) The <u>layout</u> of the document can be changed more easily using DTP than a word processor.

3) It's easy to control exactly what goes on <u>each page</u>. Word processors automatically scroll text onto the next page, which makes it difficult to do this.

This stuff is dull — bring back page 26. I WANT PAGE 26!!!

Don't worry, page 26 isn't gone forever. You see, the good thing about DTP is the way it combines everything together. DTP lets you create all sorts of documents — posters, cards, newsletters — which gives you an ideal chance to show off your fantastic images from page 26.

DTP — Working with Frames

It's the <u>frames</u> that really make <u>DTP</u> software <u>more powerful</u> than a word processor for some tasks.

Four Things You can do with a Frame

1) **PUT THEM IN COLUMNS** — most DTP software can insert <u>column guides</u> or <u>guidelines</u> (lines that appear on <u>screen</u> but not on the printed document) to help position the frames. This keeps the document looking tidy, and the layout <u>consistent</u>.

2) **LINK TEXT FRAMES TOGETHER** — so any text not fitting inside the first text frame will automatically appear inside the next one. Frames can even be linked across different pages of the document — so they're handy if you want to continue a story on a different page. This big text frame here is...

...linked to this little one here.

3) **WRAP TEXT** You can set the text to <u>wrap around</u> a picture, instead of being covered by it. This frame of text has been wrapped around a picture of a knitting sheep. (But it works with other images too — the sheep doesn't have to be knitting.)

4) **LAYERING FRAMES** i.e. putting a frame <u>on top</u> of another. E.g. you could put some text over the top of a picture. This text has been placed over a picture of a sheep playing a <u>lute</u>. (Don't worry — you can do it with images of sheep playing other instruments too.)

Templates Save Time Designing Pages

1) The <u>Golden Rule</u> of good page design applies to DTP as well as word processing — think about the <u>reader</u> and keep the page layout <u>simple</u>.

2) Most DTP software has <u>loads</u> of different templates. They <u>save time</u> but if you're not careful, documents can end up looking the <u>same</u>.

3) A template for a newspaper will have <u>columns</u>, <u>text frames</u> and <u>picture frames</u>. The text frames will be formatted with different fonts for the newspaper title, headlines and main story.

School Crest →

Text and picture frames and column guides already set up. →

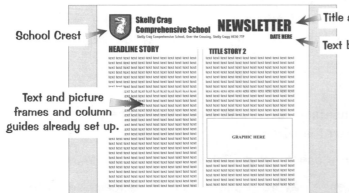

Title already formatted.

Text box to insert date.

4) You can also <u>design your own</u> template e.g. for a <u>school newsletter</u>. At the top of the template's first page you might put the school name, address, crest, and a <u>text box</u> for the date.

DTP actually stands for Daley Thompson's Pants...

It's true... Daley Thompson, the famous British decathlete in the 1984 Olympics, had the design on his shorts created using revolutionary new computer software which eventually became the desktop publishing software we know and use today. After the 1984 Olympics, IT journalists referred to the new product as the Daley Thompson Pants software which was later shortened to DTP... Actually, I made that up.

DTP — Producing a Newspaper

<u>Newspapers</u> are one of the most common places where DTP is used. When a news team are creating a page, DTP lets them jiggle the <u>layout</u> about — vital if a great story breaks at the last minute.

The News Team Collaborate to get the Job Done

The people in the team do different jobs but they're all working toward the <u>same thing</u> — finishing the paper by the <u>dreaded deadline</u>.

1. The REPORTER is the one who <u>sniffs out</u> the stories, does the <u>research</u> and <u>writes</u> the articles.

2. The articles are passed on to the SUBEDITOR — subeditors <u>proof-read</u> them and <u>check</u> the facts. Then they arrange the articles on the pages and write a <u>headline</u> for each one.

3. The PHOTOGRAPHER takes pictures that <u>illustrate</u> what the stories say.

4. The EDITOR is the <u>big boss</u> who keeps track of <u>everything</u>. They make sure everyone works together to get the paper <u>looking good</u> enough and <u>out on time</u>.

Newspapers Grab our Attention with their Layout

SNAPPY 'SPLASH'
The lead story is the most exciting bit of news — the 'splash'. Its headline is always in a big, bold font that shouts the message out in a few short words.

SUBHEADING
Sums up what the story is about. It will use the 'angle' that makes the story most exciting — so you want to read right to the end.

GRAPHICS
These are usually colourful and clear pictures that back up what's in the articles.
The best graphics are ones that could tell the story all on their own.

SPLIT INTO SECTIONS
You tend to find news stories at the front and sport at the back. Other stuff like music and film reviews comes in between — or sometimes in separate sections.

HEADLINES
Each headline explains the gist of the story that follows it — they make it easier to skim through and pick out the bits that interest you.

BODY TEXT
The main part of the story is always arranged in columns — how many depends on the paper's house style. (see below)

The Evening Zapper

INSIDE —
CAR MANIA
P12
HOROSCOPES
P24

ALIENS SPARK CANTEEN CHAOS

OUTRAGE AS THREE BOYS TURNED INTO FISHFINGERS

By Jackie German

PM's shock at boy band break-up

BYLINE
The reporter's name

House Style sets the Rules on How it Should Look

Every newspaper has its own <u>house style</u> — the set of design and writing <u>rules</u> all its team follow. The house style is tailored to suit the paper's <u>audience</u>. It includes things like the kind of <u>layout</u> and <u>fonts</u> you choose and <u>the way you write</u> — whether you use simple or long words and sentences. The house style also decides whether you write in a formal or a chatty tone.

House Style — not another DIY show, thank goodness...

If the work wasn't split into different jobs, making a paper would be rock hard. <u>Collaborating</u> makes it a lot easier — especially if the whole team follow the same set of style rules. Having a <u>house style</u> means everyone's work fits together — so it'll be a professional-looking publication.

Presentation Software

Presentation software is being used more and more by people giving <u>talks</u> or <u>displaying ideas</u>.

Presentations are used to Communicate New Information

1) <u>Presentations</u> are given either to <u>communicate</u> new information, or to help <u>persuade</u> someone of a new idea. A teacher might give a presentation to introduce a new topic in a lesson, or a salesperson could give one to persuade a group of people to buy something.

2) They can sometimes be quite <u>boring</u> — especially if the speaker just talks on and on. Presentation software can help overcome this by using multimedia and animation effects.

Presentations can be given With or Without a Speaker

1) The typical way to give a presentation is with a <u>speaker</u> introducing <u>slides</u> projected onto a large screen. The audience can read the information on the screen while the speaker gives them more detailed spoken information.

2) The other way is to give a presentation <u>without</u> a speaker. For this to work well the slides have to be good enough to communicate all the required information by themselves. <u>Multimedia</u> presentation software can help by allowing a commentary to be recorded.

Presentation Software has Four Main Features

1) Presentation software creates a series of <u>slides</u> in a single document — and each slide contains a number of <u>frames</u> (a bit like DTP software). This means that <u>text</u> and <u>images</u> — and even <u>movies</u> and <u>sounds</u> — can be put on the slide.

2) The really clever thing about presentation software is that the speaker can decide when each frame on a page appears — so each <u>bullet point</u> in a list can appear on screen at just the right moment.

3) <u>Animation effects</u> can even make the frames arrive on screen in different ways — e.g. a line of text can appear one word at a time, or the whole line can fly into place from either side.

4) The animation effects can either happen at <u>set times</u> (useful if there's no speaker), or they can be <u>controlled</u> by the speaker as he/she is talking — usually with the click of a mouse or a remote control button.

How Presentations used to be Done

1) Traditionally slides were either <u>handwritten</u> or <u>word-processed</u>.

2) Unfortunately, it's easy to muddle up the slides.

3) Another problem is that the speaker sometimes has to <u>cover up</u> information they don't want the audience to see yet.

4) Unless the speaker's very good, a presentation can easily end up looking <u>unprofessional</u>.

If you only learn one thing about presentations, learn this...

Here is a <u>**REALLY**</u> useful tip for using presentation software.
I'm going to deliver it "flying bulletpoint" style. Ready...

• ALWAYS CA

Presentation Software

It's one thing to have clever software to produce exciting slides — but it's another thing to know how to use the software to produce a good presentation. Make sure you <u>learn the following rules</u>.

Remember the Rules for Giving a Good Presentation

1) `PREPARE THOROUGHLY` — make sure you know all about the topic you're presenting. The whole point is to get people interested enough that they'll want to ask <u>questions</u> — so you need to have all the <u>answers</u>.

2) `DECIDE ON THE FORMAT` for the presentation — decide whether you'll be delivering it <u>in person</u>, or making it available as a <u>computer file</u>.

3) `WRITE THE SCRIPT` of the presentation <u>first</u> — then decide how the slides will help put the key points of the message across. The slides should be a <u>summary</u> of the main points to be made.

4) `KEEP THE SLIDES SIMPLE` — don't let background colours <u>clash</u> with the text and pictures. Ideally use the <u>same</u> background for all the slides, and don't use hard-to-read <u>fonts</u>. Use no more than <u>two</u> pictures per slide.

5) `USE OPENING AND CLOSING SLIDES` — start the presentation with an <u>attention-grabbing</u> opening slide. The closing slide should leave people with the <u>main message</u> of the presentation.

6) `KEEP EACH SLIDE'S CONTENT TO A MINIMUM` — the <u>Golden Rule</u> is to have no more than <u>six words per line</u> of text and no more than <u>five lines</u> of text on a slide. Font sizes should be big enough for people at the <u>back</u> of the audience to see — between

30 and **60** point should do.

7) `DON'T USE TOO MANY SLIDES` — if you're giving a commentary, each slide should be visible for about <u>two minutes</u>. That means no more than five main slides in a ten-minute presentation.

8) `TEST ANY ANIMATION EFFECTS` using the hardware that will be used in the <u>presentation</u>. Large movie clips might run very slowly on some systems.

9) `REHEARSE` — then rehearse, then rehearse again.

Presentation Software has Pros and Cons

ADVANTAGES OF PRESENTATION SOFTWARE

1) It produces <u>professional</u> looking presentations.

2) Use of multimedia can help <u>grab</u> and <u>keep</u> people's <u>attention</u>.

3) Presentations can be <u>saved</u> and used again — with or without the speaker being present.

4) It's easy to <u>edit</u> presentations and <u>adapt</u> them for different audiences.

DISADVANTAGES OF PRESENTATION SOFTWARE

1) It is very easy to get <u>carried away</u> by the technology and produce badly designed slides.

2) The software needs <u>expensive</u> hardware to run the presentation — a laptop computer and an LCD projector can easily cost over £3000.

It's the last page of the section — hurrah...

If you've learnt all nine rules on this page, you're ready to do your own presentation. Gulp. Scary.

Revision Summary for Section Four

This section's not just <u>amazing fun</u>, it'll also help you <u>get a job</u>. This kind of stuff goes on in offices every day. Students need to use this stuff in GCSE, A-level and University projects. And if you're really hot at it, you can convincingly doctor photographs, add amusing captions, print them out on transfers and make embarrassing T-shirts for your mates. So don't tell me this stuff isn't useful.

1) Describe two ways to highlight the text you want to edit.

2) What do these shortcuts do?
   a) CTRL X   b) CTRL Z   c) CTRL V   d) CTRL C

3) List as many ways as you can think of to make words stand out on a page.

4) What does "justifying" do? (in the context of word processing and DTP)

5) Name three things you can do with the formatting toolbar. (Careful...)

6) Why might you use a table to show lists of data (instead of writing it in one long line)?

7) Which of these things might you put in a header or footer?
   a) date   b) time   c) place   d) your phone no.   e) your photo

8) What are typos?   a) mistakes made when typing   b) mistakes made when typong

9) What is a template?

10) Describe how mail merge works.

11) What is a pixel?   a) a small coloured dot   b) a small, annoying elf-like creature

12) What's the difference between pixel-based graphics software and vector-based graphics software?

13) What is a JPEG?

14) Describe each of the following:
   a) cropping   b) grouping   c) layering

15) I've scanned a photo of Prince William, and I'd like to do the following things to the image.
   (Tick the ones you think are possible.)

   ☐   Make the picture brighter

   ☐   Make his hair blue

   ☐   Make him look like he's wrapped in plastic

   ☐   Remove him from the ski slope and put him on Rhyl beach

   ☐   Make him do a tap dance while singing "Oops... I did it again"

16) Write a mini-essay about DTP — how it works and why everyone is using it nowadays.

17) What is a template? *   * I'm talking about DTP this time, but the principle's the same
                                   so I don't mind if you "borrow" bits from your answer to Q9.
18) What does DTP stand for?
   a) Daley Thompson's Pants   b) Desk Top Publishing   c) Daley Thompson's Pants

19) Who are the four main people in a news team?

20) Describe four methods that newspapers use to grab attention on the front page.

21) List three features of presentation software.

22) List all nine rules of giving a good presentation. (Yes, I mean it.)

23) Bonus question: What are "flying bulletpoints"?

Spreadsheets — The Basics

Spreadsheets are basically pretty simple things. But they can do loads of fancy stuff, which is cool.

Spreadsheets are Clever Calculators

1) A spreadsheet is simply a program that can <u>display</u> and <u>process</u> data in a nice <u>ordered</u> way.
Most people think spreadsheets can only process numbers — but they can handle text as well.

2) Spreadsheets can: a) <u>record</u> data,   b) <u>search</u> for particular items of data,
c) do <u>calculations</u>,   d) produce <u>graphs</u> and <u>charts</u>.

3) <u>Examples</u> of uses include calculating the exam results of a group of pupils and producing graphs
based on the results of a questionnaire.

Data is Entered into Cells

1) A spreadsheet is made up of <u>rows</u> and <u>columns</u>. These divide the sheet up into individual <u>cells</u>.

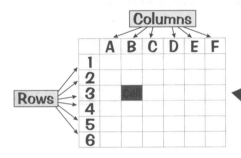

2) Each cell can be identified using the column letter
and row number as <u>coordinates</u>.

The red cell is in
Column B and Row 3 —
so its cell reference is B3.

Each Cell can contain One of Three Things

Each cell can contain <u>one</u> (and only one) of three things...

1. *Numerical data — things like numbers, dates and money.*

Most spreadsheets <u>recognise dates</u> and <u>money</u> and <u>convert</u> them into a suitable <u>format</u> — so if you enter 23-6, it's converted to 23 June.

<u>Column headings</u> usually contain text.

2. *Text data — er... words.*

You can sort text data into alphabetical order.

3. *Formulas — to add up columns, work out averages, etc.*

The great thing about spreadsheets is that if any numbers are changed, the formulas are automatically updated.

The <u>Golden Rule</u> is to put just one piece of data in a cell — don't <u>mix</u> any of these types of data.

1) If you enter a weight as '1000g' then you have <u>numerical</u> data (1000) and <u>text</u> data (g).

2) It'll treat a <u>mixed cell</u> like this as if it contains <u>only</u> text, which has a numerical value of <u>zero</u>.
This means the spreadsheet will read '1000g' as having a numerical value of <u>zero</u>. D'oh.

3) You <u>should</u> enter simply '1000' — it's <u>just numerical data</u> so everything works <u>marvellously</u>.

(The exceptions are things like currencies, where the spreadsheet knows that £5 has a value of 5.)

I tried marmite spreadsheets — but I didn't sleep so well...

Remember — numbers, words or formulas — not just a random jumble of stuff.

Spreadsheets — Simple Formulas

Without formulas, spreadsheets are just fancy tables. They really put the <u>ace</u> into 'ace spreadsheet'.

A Formula is a Simple Computer Program

1) A <u>formula</u> tells the computer to <u>process</u> data held in specific cells — using <u>functions</u> which you can either type in or select from a list.

2) The simplest <u>functions</u> are +, –, * (for <u>multiply</u>) and / (for <u>divide</u>), but there are usually loads of others, e.g. to find an <u>average</u>, or the <u>sine</u> of an angle. You can usually choose them from a list.

You're only Three Steps from Formula Heaven...

STEP 1 — Click on the cell where you want the <u>answer</u>.

STEP 2 — Type an <u>equals</u> sign (=).
(The equals sign tells the computer to expect a formula.)

STEP 3 — Type in the <u>formula</u>.
Here, it would be <u>C3+D3+E3</u>.

	A	B	C	D	E	F
	Exam Marks for 1st Year Mocks					
2	First Name	Last Name	Maths	ICT	English	Total
3	Teresa	Wood	63	45	89	=C3+D3+E3
4	Tanya	Hide	32	54	78	
5	Arthur	Brain	33	53	95	
6	Willie	Winn	24	54	75	
7	Betty	Wont	64	53	88	

Formulas can have Absolute or Relative Cell References

1) In the example above, the formula in **F3** (=C3+D3+E3) tells the computer to add together the data in the <u>three cells to the left</u>.

C	D	E	F
Maths	ICT	English	Total
63	45	89	=C3+D3+E3
32	54	78	=C4+D4+E4
33	53	95	=C5+D5+E5
24	54	75	=C6+D6+E6
64	53	88	=C7+D7+E7

2) If you <u>copy this formula</u> to cell **F4**, it <u>still</u> adds up the contents of the <u>three cells to the left</u>, so **F4** becomes '=C4+D4+E4'. These are called <u>relative</u> cell references — they use data from the same place <u>relative to the answer cell</u>.

The computer changes all the 3's to 4's, 5's, 6's and 7's when you copy and paste cell F3.

3) Sometimes part of a formula always needs to refer to <u>one particular cell</u> — and you don't want the computer to change the cell reference. In this case, you need to use an <u>absolute</u> cell reference — one that <u>won't be changed</u>.

4) The usual way to make a cell reference absolute is to put a <u>dollar sign</u> ($) in front of the cell's coordinates. So **B12** is a relative cell reference — but **B12** is an absolute cell reference.

The spreadsheet below uses an absolute cell reference
(to represent the % commission a letting agency charges on its properties).

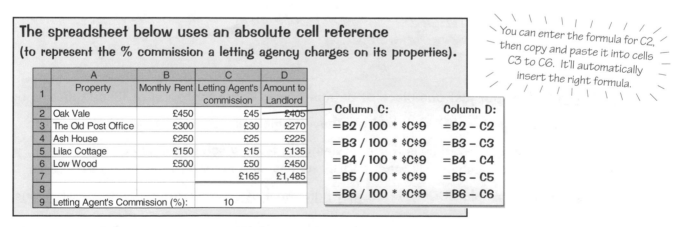

	A	B	C	D
1	Property	Monthly Rent	Letting Agent's commission	Amount to Landlord
2	Oak Vale	£450	£45	£405
3	The Old Post Office	£300	£30	£270
4	Ash House	£250	£25	£225
5	Lilac Cottage	£150	£15	£135
6	Low Wood	£500	£50	£450
7			£165	£1,485
8				
9	Letting Agent's Commission (%):		10	

Column C:
=B2 / 100 * C9
=B3 / 100 * C9
=B4 / 100 * C9
=B5 / 100 * C9
=B6 / 100 * C9

Column D:
=B2 – C2
=B3 – C3
=B4 – C4
=B5 – C5
=B6 – C6

You can enter the formula for C2, then copy and paste it into cells C3 to C6. It'll automatically insert the right formula.

Aaaarrghhh — Formulas...

Formulas always seem like they ought to be really complicated, but they're really not that bad. Programs like Microsoft Excel can do so much automatically, there's hardly any work left for you.

Spreadsheets — Graphs and Charts

Graphs and charts are different ways of communicating data in visual form.

Creating a Chart is Dead Easy...

All modern spreadsheets can produce graphs and charts.
(They all have slightly different methods, but the basic idea is always the same.)

1) Get all the data you want to show in a graph into a single block. It's best if the data is arranged in columns.

2) Highlight the data you want to use — you might need to highlight the column headings as well.

3) Select the type of chart you want.

4) Choose a good title for the chart and label any axes.

5) Decide whether the chart needs a key (also called a legend).

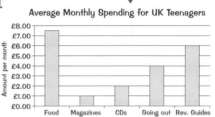

	A	B
1	Category	Monthly Spend
2	Food	£7.50
3	Magazines	£1.00
4	CDs	£2.00
5	Going out	£4.00
6	Revision Guides	£6.00

...but think about Which Type is Best

Spreadsheets can create loads of different types of graph. Sometimes it's just a matter of taste, but there are some definite rights and wrongs, so have a look at this before you pick one...

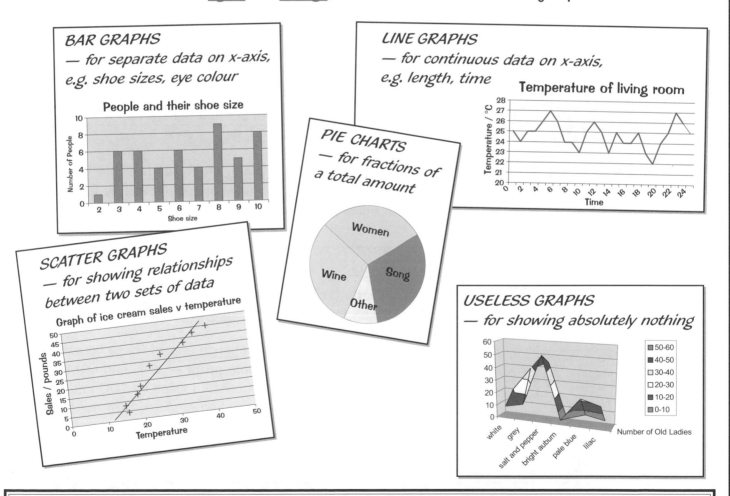

BAR GRAPHS
— for separate data on x-axis, e.g. shoe sizes, eye colour

LINE GRAPHS
— for continuous data on x-axis, e.g. length, time

SCATTER GRAPHS
— for showing relationships between two sets of data

PIE CHARTS
— for fractions of a total amount

USELESS GRAPHS
— for showing absolutely nothing

Graphs and charts — no, nothing funny about them...

Beware of picking a type of graph that's no use at all. There are some that look dead fancy, but they're not all they're cracked up to be — it's just impossible to get any information from them.

Spreadsheet Models and Simulations

Spreadsheets are dead <u>useful</u> for modelling and simulations. Here's why.

Three Reasons why Spreadsheets make Good Models

1) Spreadsheets use <u>formulas</u> to try to describe the rules that real-world things seem to follow. <u>Input values</u> can then be processed using these formulas to produce <u>output values</u>.

2) Spreadsheets can be used to carry out a <u>what-if analysis</u>. You can <u>change input values</u> to see the <u>effect</u> on the output. E.g. companies can ask a question like, "What would be the effect on profits if I invested this much money on new vehicles?"

3) The output can be <u>graphs</u> and <u>charts</u>, which make predictions of the model easier to understand.

Example 1 — Queues in a School Canteen

1) A school canteen manager could build a model to represent the relationship between the number of <u>pupils</u> wanting to eat in the canteen, the number of <u>staff</u> and the <u>queuing time</u>.

2) The model could be used to find out the number of staff needed to minimise waiting times.

	A	B
1	Number of pupils	600
2	Number of staff	4
3	Average time to serve a meal (seconds)	20
4		
5	Total serving time (minutes)	50

3) The formula in cell B5 is =B1*(B3/60)/B2. This says:

$$\text{total queuing time (in minutes)} = \frac{\text{number of pupils} \times \text{average time to serve a meal (in minutes)}}{\text{number of staff}}$$

4) A <u>weakness</u> of the model is that it assumes having <u>twice as many</u> staff will <u>halve</u> the time — it might not be that simple. It also assumes that you can have as many staff as you want — but having 100 staff would create obvious problems...

Example 2 — Profitable Pizzas

1) A pizza business could build a <u>model</u> to show its profit from selling pizzas. The owner enters data into cells B1 to B4, then the model <u>calculates</u> the data in cells B5 to B7.

	A	B
1	Production cost per pizza	£2.00
2	Other business costs	£1,000
3	Selling price per pizza	£6.00
4	Number of pizzas sold	500
5	Total costs	£2,000
6	Total profit	£1,000
7	Profit per pizza	£2.00

=B2+(B1*B4)
=(B3*B4)-B5
=B6/B4

2) The firm could <u>change</u> any of these variables to see how it affects profit — e.g. find out the effect of a reduction in sales to 400 and an increase in production costs of 50p per pizza.

3) This could be extended to give a direct link between the price of pizzas and the number sold.

Who'd've thought they'd teach you modelling at school...

Make sure you understand the examples on this page — then when you have to do one of these for yourself, you'll know exactly what to do. Won't you. You know I'm right, don't look at me like that.

Databases

Some of the basic stuff about databases was covered in the data storage section — you might want to re-read that bit before tackling this (it's on page 11).

A Database is a Store of Data

Just like stockings are used to store cats. Exactly like that, in fact.

1) A database is an organised collection of data.

2) Data is organised into fields and records.

3) The key field contains an item of data that is unique to that record — so no records have the same value in the key field. Here, the payroll number is the key field.

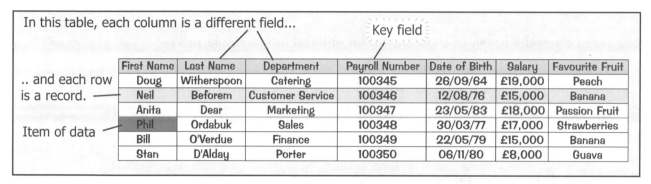

In this table, each column is a different field...   Key field

.. and each row is a record.

Item of data

First Name	Last Name	Department	Payroll Number	Date of Birth	Salary	Favourite Fruit
Doug	Witherspoon	Catering	100345	26/09/64	£19,000	Peach
Neil	Beforem	Customer Service	100346	12/08/76	£15,000	Banana
Anita	Dear	Marketing	100347	23/05/83	£18,000	Passion Fruit
Phil	Ordabuk	Sales	100348	30/03/77	£17,000	Strawberries
Bill	O'Verdue	Finance	100349	22/05/79	£15,000	Banana
Stan	D'Alday	Porter	100350	06/11/80	£8,000	Guava

4) The big benefit of databases is that you can search them quickly to find specific data, or use them to generate reports — e.g. which books in a publisher's database have sold the most.

Well-Structured Fields are Really Important

1) The first step in creating a database is to decide on what fields you need. And once you've decided that, each field needs a name, a description of its contents, a data type and a format.

2) The data type is dead important, as different processes can be performed on different types of data. The most common data types are in the box — most programs allow others.

TEXT e.g. Banana
INTEGERS i.e. whole numbers such as 25
REAL NUMBERS e.g. 25.67
DATES e.g. 26-09-82 or 26/09/82

3) One way to reduce the file size of the database is to use coding. E.g. use 'M' and 'F' for gender instead of 'male' and 'female'. This uses fewer characters and so takes up less memory.

Databases — nope, drawing a blank there as well...

The thing is — this is really dull stuff. But you've got to learn it, see. So I'm just going to prattle on about it for a couple more lines in the hope that some of it'll stick... actually, I'm not doing too well, am I — just prattling on about prattling on really. I think I'll stop now. That's probably best.

Revision Summary for Section Five

If you ever get a job in an office, i'll bet you a fiver you'll need to use a spreadsheet at some point. There's nothing too tricky about them — just make sure you can do these questions and you'll have the basics down pat. "Down pat"? I wonder where that came from — it's a really weird thing to write, now I come to think of it. Hmmm ... you know what I mean, though.

1) What is the smallest part of a spreadsheet called?
 a) Sell b) Smell c) Cell

2) Which row is cell G14 in?

3) How many different types of data should be entered into a single cell?

4) If you want to put the distance 16,000 miles into a spreadsheet, what should you type?

5) Is C6 an absolute or a relative cell reference?

6) What does "absolute cell reference" mean?

7) How easy is it to create a chart in a spreadsheet?
 a) Dead easy b) Dead easy c) Dead easy

8) Pick a suitable chart to show the relationship between time of day and temperature.

9) Give an example of something you could show with a pie chart.

10) What's a "what-if analysis" when it's at home?

11) What does this formula mean?: Write it in "normal maths". Then work out the value that will appear in cell C3.

	A	B	C	D	E
1	3	6	9		
2	4	8	12		
3					

=A1*(B2 – A2)/C2

12) What formula will Farmer Kevin put into cell B5?

13) What is a database?

	A	B
1	Cow	Selling price
2	Daisy	£48.26
3	Buttercup	£58.69
4	Boris	£2.50
5	Total income	

14) What is a key field?

15) What might be the key field in a database listing information about different books?

16) How could you reduce the file size of a database?

Internet Basics

The Internet is becoming more and more important all the time — ignore it at your own risk.

You need a Modem and a Browser to get on the Internet

1) Most people use a PC and a normal telephone line to access the Internet.
The computer is attached to the telephone line with a modem.
A modem converts computer signals to signals that can be carried over telephone lines.
(And it also converts signals from the telephone line to signals a computer can understand.)

2) To connect to the Internet, you use your modem to dial up a computer owned by an Internet Service Provider (ISP). An ISP is a company that has computers permanently connected to the Internet. All the information sent from your PC goes through the ISP's computer.

3) The two most important pieces of software you need are a web browser to display web pages, and an e-mail client, which transmits and receives e-mail.

The Internet has Two Main Parts

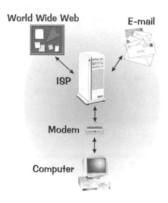

1) The World Wide Web (WWW) is the part that contains web pages.
It's like an enormous notice board — people put things onto the
Web and then other people can read them.

2) Electronic Mail (E-mail) is the part where messages are sent from
one person to another — it works a bit like sending a letter, but
it's much quicker. (For more about e-mail, see page 48.)

You Need to Know Lots about the Internet

Since the Internet is pretty important, you should know quite a lot about it.
Especially these three things...

1) RESEARCH

Maybe you've got to do a boring history project
— or maybe you just want to find out everything you can
about Swiss cheese (I know I do)...

Either way, there's loads of information on the Internet,
and you need to know how to find the useful stuff.

Telling the whole world
about something used
to be much trickier.

2) MAKING A WEB PAGE

This sounds pretty hard, but it's not as bad as
all that. Just think — you can tell the world
everything about anything you're interested in.

3) USING E-MAIL

This is as easy as falling off a giant horse that keeps bucking and jumping about all the time.
And it's as useful as a giant history homework machine.

Surfing the web — take a towel for afterwards...

The Internet looks as though it's all dead complicated. Well, it's more complicated than a
jam sandwich, that's for sure. But it shouldn't be too hard to get your head round if you really try.

Researching a Topic

You're in a boring geography lesson and teacher asks you to find out everything you can about Mongolia for next lesson. No need to panic — there's <u>lots</u> of places you can look.

Get Information from Books, CD-ROMs and the Internet

These are the <u>obvious</u> places to start looking for information.

BOOKS	CD-ROMs	THE INTERNET
The Internet has moving pictures, but you don't need lots of expensive gear to read a book, and it's easy to carry round with you.	These contain as much information as a load of books, and you don't risk running up a big telephone bill.	It contains as much information as a load of trucks full of books. In fact, there's so much information, it can be a right pain in the neck finding the stuff you need.

Find Stuff on the Internet using a Search Engine

The most obvious way to start looking for information on the Internet is with a <u>search engine</u>. <u>Search engines</u> are websites that help you search for other websites.

1) Usually you type in a <u>keyword</u> and the search engine lists a load of websites containing that keyword.

2) You can do a <u>complex</u> search using more than one keyword and linking them together with <u>AND</u> and <u>OR</u>.

Some Popular Search Engines are...

Google   Lycos

Yahoo   AltaVista

Ask Jeeves   Excite

Different Search Engines produce Different Results

1) Most search engines work by storing <u>keywords</u> of different websites. When you search, you usually get a <u>list</u> of possible web pages (or '<u>hits</u>') with your keyword in.

2) The list of hits can be very <u>long</u> — but usually the search engine just shows you 10 or 20 hits at a time. You have to click a button to see the next 20 hits, and the next 20 and so on.

3) No search engine will have data on <u>every</u> website — so different search engines will often produce different hits.

4) This means it's worth using <u>more than one</u> search engine when you're looking for something.

Boo-Hoo   **Search Engine**   **Go**

You searched for: seal

Hits 1 - 20 of 600,000,000,000 are shown below

1. Creatures of the oceans
A website devoted to ocean stuff.
www.underwaterstuff.com

2. Yeti mystery solved?
Is the mysterious Yeti actually a seal?
www.completelymadeup.co.uk

The List of Hits tells you Something about Each Page

1) The list of hits from a search engine gives you a <u>few details</u> about each site.

2) It usually gives you the <u>title</u> of a web page, plus a <u>short description</u> of the site.

3) It also tells you the <u>URL</u> (or web <u>address</u>) of the site.

Example: http://www.cgpbooks.co.uk/whatsnew.htm

This is the <u>URL</u> of the CGP "What's New" web page.

You have to type URLs very carefully, with all the <u>full stops</u>, <u>colons</u> and <u>slashes</u> in the right places — otherwise they don't work. Hurumph.

A list of hits — The Beatles must be at Number 1...

Just because the Internet's new and exciting, it doesn't mean that it's better than the good old-fashioned book for everything. It's often much quicker just to look it up in an encyclopaedia.

Searching for Information

A list of hits might have <u>millions</u> of websites on it — it could take <u>years</u> to look at all of them. You need to pick out the ones that are <u>most likely</u> to be useful.

Start at the Top of your List of Hits

It's a good idea to have some kind of <u>system</u> when you're searching the Internet.

1) Look at the details about <u>number 1</u> in your list <u>first</u>, then <u>number 2</u>, and so on. Don't look at number 7 first, then number 3, then number 5 and so on — you'll just get confused (and it's a pretty daft idea anyway, when you think about it).

2) You don't always have to <u>visit</u> the website to know that a result is <u>useless</u> — just looking at the page's URL can give you some idea.

3) The URL gives you some idea of who <u>wrote</u> the page — this is sometimes enough to know that it <u>won't</u> be very helpful.

> **Yee-har...** Search... New search
>
> *You searched for...* | Cheddar |
>
> **Results 1 - 10 of 81315**
>
> 1. Cheddar Gorge
>   Come and see the caves of
>   Cheddar Gorge
>   www.cheddargorgecave.co.uk
>
> 2. Cheddar cheese
>   Oh, what a lovely piece of cheese
>   www.cheese.co.uk

> I wanted to find out about cheddar cheese, so I searched for cheddar on this search engine.
>
> It's pretty obvious the first result isn't going to help (looks like it's about Cheddar Gorge cave), so I won't bother looking at that.

Use the Back and Forward Buttons

1) If a site looks as though it might be <u>useful</u>, click on the <u>link</u> for a proper look.

2) It might be useless — if so, you can just click on your browser's '<u>Back</u>' button to go back to where you were before.

3) The <u>back</u> and <u>forward</u> buttons are great — you can 'retrace your steps' to go back to a page you saw earlier, and then go forwards again if you like.

4) But if a site turns out to be useful, you might want to follow <u>hyperlinks</u> to <u>trail your idea</u>. Each link might take you to another useful web page.

5) Hyperlinks are often coloured <u>blue</u> and <u>underlined</u>, and are usually displayed in a different colour (like red) if you've followed them before.

> <u>Hyperlinks</u> are the bits on a web page that you can click on to go somewhere else.
>
> The pointer changes to a <u>hand</u> when you hover over a hyperlink.

Web browsers have Other Features to Help you Navigate

BOOKMARKS

Browsers can <u>save</u> URLs you use often, so you don't have to type them — a feature called '<u>bookmarks</u>' or '<u>favourites</u>'.

You can save bookmarks in <u>groups</u>. This makes it easier to find the one you want — e.g. you might want to put all your favourite cheese websites together.

HISTORY

Browsers usually keep a list of all the websites you've visited — this is called the <u>history</u>. If you want to go back to a website, you can get the URL from the history list.

Hyperlinks — useful, though not very funny...

Web browsers usually try to make life easy for you. The best way to find out how to use a web browser properly is to read this page, find a computer, and then have a go yourself. Trust me.

Searching for Information

If a website has information you want to use, you need to <u>save</u> it so you can use it later. But first, you need to <u>find</u> those interesting bits.

Find the Interesting bits

1) If you find a website that you reckon might have some useful information, it can be a good idea to find an <u>index</u>, a <u>list of contents</u> or a <u>site map</u>.

2) A <u>list of contents</u> or a <u>site map</u> shows how the website is organised — see page 47 for more about website structure.

3) You might need to '<u>scan</u>' a web page that looks interesting — read it all <u>really quickly</u> so you understand basically what it's about.

4) Or if you're interested in information about, say, 'fluff', you might want to find the word 'fluff' wherever it appears on the page.

5) You can use the browser's '<u>Find</u>' option to do this — just go to the <u>Edit</u> menu and it should be on there.

Copy and Paste the Stuff you want to Keep

1) When you find an interesting bit of <u>text</u>, or a good <u>picture</u>, you'll probably want to <u>save</u> it.

2) Use the <u>File</u> menu to save the whole page. (Some older browsers don't save the graphics this way.)

3) Instead of saving the <u>whole</u> page, or printing it <u>all</u> out, you can just keep the bits you <u>need</u>.

4) <u>Highlight</u> any text you want to keep, then <u>copy</u> it and <u>paste</u> it into a word processor document. Pasting all the good stuff into one document is a pretty convenient thing to do.

5) If you find a good picture, <u>right click</u> on it — you should be able to <u>copy</u> it and <u>paste</u> it into a graphics program (or maybe a word processor).

Keep a Log of what you Find

1) When you save something from the Web, it's best to make a note of the <u>URL</u> where you found it.

2) Then if you use it, you can tell other people where you got it. If you <u>don't</u> do this, you're being <u>jolly naughty</u>.

3) The easiest way to keep a note of where you found things is to <u>copy</u> the website address from the <u>Address Bar</u>.

4) <u>Paste</u> the address underneath the information you've taken from that page.

This is the <u>Address Bar</u>. You can cut the URL from here...

...and paste it in another document.

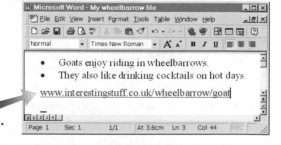

Find the interesting bits — buy a different book...

It sounds kind of obvious that you need to remember exactly where you found that really interesting fact about belly button fluff. But it's all too easy to forget in the excitement...

Fact and Opinion

Anyone can put information on the Internet, which means a lot of the stuff that's there is just plain untrue. And if it's not exactly untrue, there's a chance it might be biased.

Biased Information Supports a Particular Point of View

1) All the information on the Internet has been written by people (probably).
   This means that the information could be 'biased'.

2) Information that's biased supports a particular point of view without being completely fair.
   Perhaps some facts are ignored because they don't fit in with the writer's opinion.

3) People often claim biased opinions to be facts, even when they're not facts at all.
   You need to be careful.

People can be Biased for Lots of Reasons

1) There are a shed full of reasons why a person might be biased.

2) People might write a biased article or provide biased information because they want to support a particular political party.

I say fox hunting's cruel.

And I say it isn't.

3) Or they might want to convince other people to believe the same as they do — e.g. some people say that fox hunting is cruel, others say that it isn't.

4) If more people support their argument, it's more likely that politicians and other people will help them.

Primary Data is Turned into Secondary Data

1) Some information on the Internet is primary data — this means that no one has 'interpreted' the results yet. An example of this would be readings from temperature sensors in various places around the world.

M6
Birmingham 42
London 124

I say the world is definitely getting colder.

2) People 'interpret' this primary data — they write down what they think the data is saying. This is then called secondary data, and is what you usually see on the news and in newspapers.

Daily Nonsense
PHONE POLL REVEALS
100% OF PEOPLE NOW OWN A TELEPHONE
Win a wheelbarrow

3) Different people often interpret primary data in different ways. They might claim the same data's saying completely different things.

4) For example, some people might use data to say that the Earth is getting warmer. But others will use the same data to claim that the Earth is heading for another ice age. It all comes down to interpretation — and bias.

5) Statistics are definitely ones to watch — they can be very misleading.

I'm bi-assed — I've got two mules...

Bias — it's tricky. No one will admit that they're biased, but pretty much everyone is (except me, that's for sure). Anyway, it's worth questioning whether things you read could be biased.

Design a Web Page

You don't have to read other people's web pages — you can make <u>your own</u> easily enough...

Well-designed Websites follow Five Golden Rules

Websites need to be <u>interesting</u> to read, just like a newspaper or a book.
But there are a few <u>extra</u> things you need to think about as well...

① **CLEAR** A nice background colour can make the page look lovely.
But keep backgrounds <u>simple</u>, and choose text colours that stand out clearly so that the information is easy to read.

② **SIMPLE** Keep the overall design <u>simple</u> — and use a <u>similar</u> layout on all the pages, so it's <u>easier</u> to navigate through the site. Also, you need to make it dead clear what all the buttons link to.

③ **PICTURES** <u>Pictures</u> make a web page more interesting. But only use graphics you really <u>need</u> — they can take a <u>long time</u> to download.

④ **LINKS** Keep the number of <u>hyperlinks</u> needed to reach anywhere to a <u>minimum</u>. Ideally, it shouldn't take someone more than <u>three</u> links to get to anywhere on your website.

⑤ **FONTS** It's best not to use too many <u>different fonts</u> on a page — it looks a bit untidy. Use a small number of fonts, and just make titles and other stuff that needs to stand out <u>bigger</u> or <u>bold</u>.

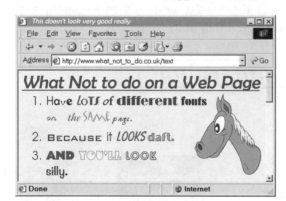

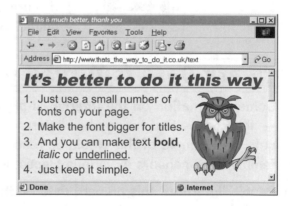

Different People will be interested in Different Links

Web pages aren't like books — with a book you start at page 1, and read all the pages <u>in order</u> until you finish. Web pages have buttons so you can <u>choose</u> what you want to read.

1) You can have lots of <u>buttons</u> or <u>hyperlinks</u> on your web page, all linking to different pages.

2) This is pretty handy, as <u>different people</u> will be interested in <u>different things</u>.

Click on the link that interests <u>you</u>...
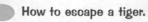 How to catch a deer.
How to escape a tiger.

See page 47 for more about designing a website.

Five golden rules — 4 mocking birds, 3 French hens, 2 turtle doves...

You want as many people as possible to read your web pages, and the way to do that is to make your site look good, and be as easy to read and use as possible. That's how the best sites do it.

Creating a Web Page

It's best to use special <u>web-design</u> software for this — but a decent <u>word processor</u> might be okay. Whatever you use, the basics will be pretty much the same.

Easy stuff — Headings and Text

If you're using a word processor to make a web page, you can only use the more <u>basic</u> features. Basically, this is because HTML (see page 46) is quite limited.

You can change the formatting of <u>whole</u> <u>paragraphs</u> (by choosing a paragraph style)...

...or just of highlighted <u>words</u>.

| Normal ▼ | Times New Roman ▼ | A⁺ A⁻ | **B** *I* <u>U</u> |

There are a few other <u>easy</u> things you can do as well — check out the <u>Format</u> menu.

1. Changing the <u>background</u> is as simple as choosing a colour or a picture.
2. Different kinds of <u>list</u> are easy...
3. ...and horizontal lines are no problem at all — use the <u>Insert</u> menu.

This is a nice big heading
This is just <u>normal</u> text, so it's a bit smaller.
- It's a piece of cake to make a <u>bulleted list</u>.
- Like this one.
1. Or a <u>numbered list</u>.
2. Use the Format menu, or these <u>buttons</u>.

Harder stuff — Tables and Pictures

Tables Because of the way HTML works, <u>positioning</u> things on screen often involves making a <u>table</u>.

Celebrities' Favourite Vegetables
Julia Roberts	Potato	
Madonna	Peas	
Clark Kent	Tomato	

1) I'm making this website about vegetables, and I want to put the information in <u>columns</u>.
2) I don't want a table to appear on screen — but it's the <u>easiest</u> way to put everything in the right place.
3) I can then make the lines in the table <u>invisible</u>.

Pictures
1) Adding <u>pictures</u> is easy enough — just click on the <u>Image</u> button.
2) Getting pictures to appear in the right place is tricky at first. But it's easy when you know the secret — use a <u>table</u>.

Use tables to position pictures where you need them.

Different Kinds of picture — GIFs and JPEGs
- The two main types of picture used on the Internet are <u>GIFs</u> and <u>JPEGs</u>.
- GIF files are best for simple pictures with <u>few colours</u> — such as <u>logos</u> and simple <u>line drawings</u>. GIFs can also have <u>transparent</u> areas, where the web page's background colour will show through.
- JPEG files are better for <u>photographs</u>, as they can display far more colours than a GIF.
- To <u>convert</u> between the two types, <u>open</u> your graphic in a graphics program, and '<u>Save As</u>' the other type.

Don't rush me — I'll be with you in a GIF-fy...

Tables are a godsend when you're making a web page. If you're having problems with the layout of your web page, a table will probably help. And you can always make the lines invisible.

Creating a Web Page — the Harder Bits

When you're bored with the easy stuff, you can add all sorts of complicated things.
Think about it — <u>links</u> and <u>animations</u>... yowzers.

Make a link in Two Easy Steps

Making a <u>link</u> to other files or web pages involves three pretty easy steps.

1) You create the <u>word</u>, <u>shape</u> or <u>picture</u> that you want to use as the button.

2) Then you <u>select</u> the button and make it a <u>link</u> by clicking on the <u>hyperlink button</u>.

3) Finally, type the <u>address</u> of the page you want to link to in the box marked '<u>URL</u>'.

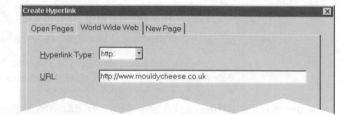

Create Animations — Make Stuff Move

It's fairly easy to create <u>animated GIFs</u>. They're a bit like cartoons — a series of pictures is shown one after the other very quickly so that it looks as though something is <u>moving</u>.

Each frame is slightly different to the one before.

 Mr. R Cake (the history teacher) dances frame by frame.

1) First you make the individual pictures, called '<u>frames</u>' — most graphics programs can save files as GIFs (which is what you need here).

2) Once you've made all the separate frames, you need a special piece of software that can combine them into a kind of 'cartoon' — a good <u>graphics program</u> might have this already.

3) You choose <u>which frames</u> to include, their <u>order</u>, their <u>speed</u>, and <u>how many times</u> you want the animation to run.

4) Then the program makes the <u>animated GIF</u>.

Animated GIFs are a <u>compromise</u> between <u>file size</u> and <u>image quality</u> — smaller files are better, but their quality is lower. If you want better images, that means increasing the file size.

Everything gets Converted to HTML

<u>HTML</u> is the language of the World Wide Web — but it's dead complicated. Luckily, <u>web-design</u> software means you can produce HTML pages without knowing anything about HTML.

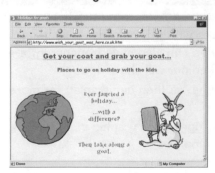

Take a simple web page...

...click on the 'View' menu, and choose 'Source'...

...and you can see what it looks like in HTML.

HTML — <metajoke> Content = "too hard" </metajoke>...

HTML is a mess, but all web pages need to be in HTML. Sounds like it could be a problem — but not if you have web-design software. Just design away and leave HTML to the computer.

Design a Website

If everybody else can have their own website, then you might as well have one too. But there's quite a lot to think about <u>before</u> you start writing pages.

Use a Spider Chart to Organise your Site

This <u>spider chart</u> shows all the pages in my exciting new website, and how they <u>link together</u>.

1) It's definitely worth drawing this kind of diagram <u>before</u> you start making any pages.

2) It'll help avoid getting <u>confused</u> later.

3) Different <u>structures</u> are possible — choose something that makes sense for <u>your</u> website.

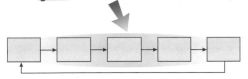

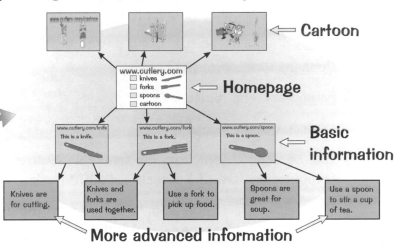

Cartoon

Homepage

Basic information

More advanced information

Don't go round Upsetting People

People can be easily upset by things on websites, so you need to be careful you're not doing anything <u>dodgy</u>.

Libel means telling Damaging Lies

1) <u>Libelling</u> someone means publishing something <u>untrue</u> about them that <u>damages</u> their <u>reputation</u>.

2) There are '<u>libel laws</u>' to stop people doing this. Newspapers have been taken to court and been forced to pay <u>thousands</u> of pounds for publishing untrue things about people.

Show a bit of Sensitivity towards Others

If Andy has a <u>big nose</u>, and doesn't really like it, he might be a bit upset if you made a website called "<u>www.andyhasabighooter.com</u>". Think about what you're saying.

Don't Copy Things and Say You Wrote Them
Clearly naughty.

Plagiarism means Copying

<u>Plagiarism</u> is when you <u>copy</u> what someone else has written or said, and say that <u>you</u> thought of it first. It's very naughty. It's like copying someone else's homework. But worse.

Acknowledge Other People's Work

1) If you're going to use what <u>someone else</u> has written on your website, you need to <u>acknowledge</u> (i.e. say) that they wrote it first.

2) This is because they own the <u>copyright</u> on what they've written — i.e. they 'own' what they wrote.

Homepage Front — the website makeover program...
Should be pretty obvious — don't upset people and don't copy stuff. If you upset the wrong person, they'll take you to court and you might have to pay £20,000,000,000,000. Scary.

E-Mail

E-mail's fairly useful really — that's why nearly everybody uses it. And that's a good reason why you should want to know about it, I reckon.

Five Steps to Sending an E-Mail

Electronic mail (e-mail) is a way of sending messages (and documents) from one computer to another. You can even use some mobile phones or a digital television to send e-mail.

STEP 1: Create the message e.g. using a word processor or the e-mail software on a computer.

STEP 2: Connect to the Internet.

STEP 3: Press the 'send' button.

...then the machines take over...

> Web-based e-mail is when you don't have to be connected to a particular ISP to send and receive e-mail. You just have to go to a certain website — like 'hotmail', for example. With web-based e-mail, you do step 2 before step 1.

STEP 4: The message is sent from the sender's ISP to a special place in memory in the computer system of the recipient's ISP (called the 'mailbox').

STEP 5: The recipient later connects to the Internet, opens their e-mail account, and finds the new message — which they then download and open.

Take Care Opening Attachments

1) It's also possible to send files via e-mail — these are called attachments. For example, you could e-mail a picture or a music file to a friend.

2) Unless you're expecting to receive an attachment, treat any you receive with suspicion — it's easy to get a virus from an infected attachment. Viruses are covered on page 10.

3) It's possible to view an attachment without fully downloading it, or you can use virus-checking software to scan it before downloading. Both help to reduce the risk of getting a virus.

> The golden rule is never open an attachment unless you know who sent it.

E-Mail has Benefits and Problems

E-mail PROS	E-mail CONS
1) It's quick — e-mails take seconds to send, compared to days for a letter.	1) The sender and receiver both need Internet access and e-mail accounts.
2) It's cheap — e-mails are cheaper than posting or faxing.	2) The hardware and software needed is expensive if you just need e-mail.
3) The same message can easily be sent to loads of different people — and if you group addresses, sending a message to lots of people is as easy as sending it to one person.	3) Get a single letter of an e-mail address wrong, and the message won't be delivered.
	4) The message will sit in the recipient's mailbox until they next look at their e-mail account.

My mate's got loads of insect friends — he gets loads of flea-mails...

The best way to get to know about e-mail isn't by reading a book, it's by e-mailing people. So get your friends' e-mail addresses, and tell them all your news. Or your favourite joke or something.

Address Books

Just like you keep your friends' home addresses in an address book, you can keep e-mail addresses in an e-mail <u>address book</u>. They're handy old things, and easy to use.

Address Books are Lists of E-mail Addresses

1) This is my e-mail <u>address book</u>.

2) It's just a <u>list</u> of e-mail addresses.

3) That's it — nothing fancy at all.

Add New Addresses by Right-Clicking

If someone sends you an e-mail, you might want to <u>add</u> their e-mail address to your <u>address book</u>. Then you'll be able to contact them later.

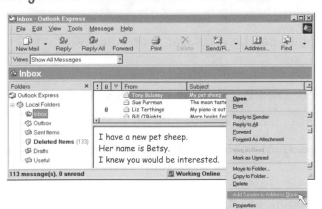

1) I've just <u>received</u> this message from Tony Baloney — his e-mail address is <u>baloney@dearserve.co.uk</u>.

2) To <u>add</u> his address to my address book, I can just <u>right-click</u> on the message and choose 'Add sender to Address Book'.

3) Other e-mail software might work <u>slightly</u> differently, but you'll be able to do the <u>same thing</u>.

Make Distribution Lists using Groups

Say you want to send one e-mail to all the people you <u>like</u>, and a different e-mail to all the people you <u>don't like</u>. You could sit down and type all the e-mails separately, but there's an easier way.

1) You can make two <u>Groups</u> — one called '<u>Like</u>' and the other called '<u>Dislike</u>'.

2) The <u>group</u> called 'Like' will have the <u>e-mail</u> addresses of all the people you like in it.

3) But 'Like' also has its <u>own</u> e-mail address — you can send an e-mail to 'Like'.

4) When you send an e-mail to 'Like', the e-mail goes to <u>all</u> the people in the group. This means you can type an e-mail <u>once</u>, but send it to <u>loads</u> of different people.

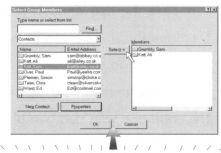

Choose an e-mail address you want to add to the group and click on 'Select'.

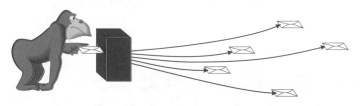

This is kind of how groups work — you post one letter but it goes to loads of people.

Distribution lists — handy at Christmas...

This page is as easy as finding a haystack in a big pile of needles. The only bit that's even a little bit tricky is the stuff about groups of e-mail addresses. And that's not hard. So stop moaning.

Revision Summary for Section Six

What a lovely section that was. Of course, it's not over yet — there's still these juicy questions to come. Try your hand at these little devils, and see how you do. If there's stuff you don't know, go back and have a look at the section, and then try the questions again. Keep doing this until you can answer all the questions without getting any wrong. Then you'll know you've learnt something.

1) Explain why you might need a modem to connect to the Internet.

2) Describe why the following two pieces of software are useful:
   a) a web browser   b) an e-mail client.

3) What are the two main parts of the Internet called?

4) Describe one way to look for information on the Internet.

5) Why do different search engines produce different lists of hits?

6) Explain what a URL is.

7) Explain what a hyperlink is and what it does.

8) Explain how web pages that have already been visited can be displayed more quickly.

9) What is found in a history folder?

   a) a plan of the Battle of Hastings   b) history coursework   c) links to recently visited websites

10) Describe 3 things you might find on a website that could tell you what's on that site.

11) Describe one way to make sure you don't forget any interesting stuff you find on the Internet.

12) What is biased information?

13) Explain the difference between primary data and secondary data.

14) Give five rules of good website design.

15) Describe one way to make a website useful for different kinds of people.

16) Describe one way to make laying out a web page easy.

17) What are the two kinds of picture commonly used on the Internet? How are they different?

18) Describe the three steps in making a hyperlink.

19) Explain how to create an animated GIF.

20) What programming language are web pages written in?

21) Describe one way you can plan how all the pages on your website will link together.

22) What is meant by: a) libel   b) plagiarism   c) copyright?

23) Explain fully how an e-mail is sent and then read by the recipient.

24) What are attachments? Describe one potential problem with opening attachments.

25) Explain three benefits and four problems of using e-mail.

26) What is an e-mail address book?

27) Explain why it's useful to make 'groups' of e-mail addresses.

Computers in Shops

This section covers pretty much all the applications of ICT you need to know about. But there are loads more than this. Shoploads, in fact.

A Bar code Stores Information about the Product

1) Bar codes are these things:  ⟵ a barcode

2) You find bar codes on most products — like tins of beans, clothes labels, and the back of this book. A bar code contains details about the product.

> All bar codes end with a check digit, so the computer can validate that the data is correct.

3) EPOS stands for Electronic Point of Sale — the fancy high-tech tills in supermarkets and places. The bar code details are scanned into the system by a laser scanner on the till. This is connected to the store's computer system, which contains the current price of the product. The price is passed back to the till, which processes and prints the customer's bill and receipt.

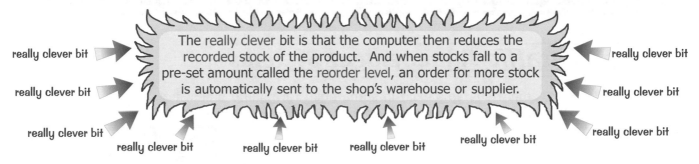

really clever bit → really clever bit → really clever bit →

really clever bit → really clever bit → really clever bit →

← really clever bit ← really clever bit ← really clever bit

really clever bit

The really clever bit is that the computer then reduces the recorded stock of the product. And when stocks fall to a pre-set amount called the reorder level, an order for more stock is automatically sent to the shop's warehouse or supplier.

Debit Cards Reduce the Need for Cash

Excuse me — is it OK to pay by card here?

1) Most tills allow customers to pay for their shopping using a debit card instead of cash. This is called Electronic Funds Transfer at the Point of Sale — or EFTPOS for short.

2) Debit cards have a magnetic stripe (or strip) on the back of them. They're read by swiping the card through a magnetic reader, which tells the computer which bank account the money will come from.

3) A request for the payment is then automatically sent via the telephone network. If the card is valid, the payment is authorised, and the funds are transferred from the customer's account to the shop's.

```
Dog chew       0.45
Dog basket    19.99
Dg fd mlt 12s  6.50

Total:        26.94
Swatch
0000 0000 0000 0000 000
Ex 05/04
Swiped
Issue 3

Sale
AMOUNT        26.94
Please debit my account

Thank you. Please keep this
receipt for your records.
```

"That seems to be in order. Thank you Mr McMannon."

4) The card has a space for the customer to put their signature to reduce the risk of card fraud — paying for goods using someone else's card. The card is checked against the signature the customer puts onto the receipt. Both the customer and the shop keep a copy of the receipt.

Winning the Lottery — that reduces your need for cash...

It's funny, I never even think about all the stuff that goes on behind the scenes when I'm buying my food. All the wonders of modern technology. Yep, it's really strange, that.

More Computer Applications

A load of examples of ICT uses — make sure you know <u>how the ICT works</u> and the <u>benefits</u> of it.

Loyalty Cards Find Out What Each Shopper Buys

1) Some large shops such as supermarkets have introduced <u>loyalty cards</u>. These contain details of the customer and their <u>loyalty scheme</u> account number. The loyalty card is swiped when the customer buys something, and <u>details of their purchases</u> are <u>stored</u> on the computer system.

SPECIAL OFFER
WIGS
50% EXTRA FREE
Offer lasts until 23rd April 2001

2) The customer is usually '<u>rewarded</u>' with <u>discounts</u> and <u>vouchers</u> when their spending rises above a certain level. But there's <u>another reason</u> for loyalty cards...

3) The shop's <u>customer database</u> is <u>linked</u> to the <u>product-sales database</u> by the loyalty scheme account number. This way the store knows <u>exactly</u> what each customer has bought. They can use this information to <u>stock</u> more of <u>popular goods</u>, and send <u>personalised mailshots</u> — e.g. someone who buys dog biscuits every week could be told about an offer on flea collars.

Cars and Traffic Management Systems

1) Car park <u>management systems</u> exist in some <u>busy towns</u> and cities, e.g. Exeter.

2) <u>Sensors</u> at the <u>entrances</u> and <u>exits</u> of <u>car parks</u> are used to calculate how many <u>spaces</u> are left in each car park.

> WELCOME TO EXETER.
> ALL PARKING SPACES ARE FULL.
> PLEASE PARK IN WALES.

3) This data is sent to <u>signs</u> next to nearby roads, which <u>update</u> their display in <u>real time</u>. Which means motorists shouldn't have to <u>waste time</u> driving to a car park that's <u>already full</u>.

Modern Weather Forecasting needs ICT

For more on data logging, see page 54.

1) <u>Meteorological data</u> such as rainfall or air pressure is usually collected from an automated <u>data-logging</u> system using <u>sensors</u>. The data is either <u>sent</u> straight to a central computer, or <u>stored</u> within the data-logging device before being downloaded.

2) The data is processed to produce a <u>weather map</u> of the area using a <u>geographical information system</u>.

3) A series of images collected at different times can also be used to create a kind of <u>moving image</u> of the <u>weather systems</u>. The same can be done for data collected by a weather <u>satellite</u>.

4) The data can also be fed into a <u>computer model</u> of the way weather patterns change — to make a more detailed weather forecast. In this way <u>more data</u> can be analysed than with a manual system. The predictions are also more <u>accurate</u>.

It certainly beats "it's going to rain, I can feel it in my bones"...

I know, I know... loyalty cards don't exactly get the pulse racing, but you need to know why they caught on. I mean, they're <u>everywhere</u> now — they must be quite important to the supermarkets.

Even More Computer Applications

Pretty much everywhere you look nowadays there's a computer involved. So in today's page, boys and girls, I'll be showing you two more applications of computers in the real world.

Electronic Kiosks for Tourist Information and Tickets...

Electronic kiosks are becoming quite <u>popular</u> — things like <u>ticket machines</u> are fairly commonplace, but you also get <u>information points</u> in museums, <u>tourist information centres</u> and <u>train stations</u>. There's one at <u>Lancaster</u>.

There are <u>two</u> basic types:

1 **POINT OF SALE**
This is a kind of <u>vending machine</u>.

> E.g. ticket machines at stations and airports — you go through the options till you get to the ticket you want, then stick in your money and it prints a ticket for you. Grand.

2 **POINT OF INFORMATION**
This is a <u>multimedia device</u> for providing <u>information</u>.

> E.g. tourist information centres and train stations provide information about nearby tourist attractions.
> Museums also use them to provide extra information — they're supposed to be "more fun for the kids".

Excuse me dear... You there in the red... What time's the bingo bus?

These kiosks can be <u>really simple</u> or <u>really fancy</u> — some can run <u>video sequences</u> and all sorts. They often use <u>touch-screen technology</u>, where you press or <u>touch the screen</u> to choose <u>options</u>.

Gantt Diagrams make it Easy to Manage a Project

1) A <u>Gantt diagram</u> is a kind of <u>schedule</u> for working out <u>how long</u> a <u>project</u> will <u>take</u>.

2) You break down the project into <u>specific tasks</u> and input how long <u>each task</u> will take.

3) What you get out (the output) is a <u>schedule</u> that looks something like this:

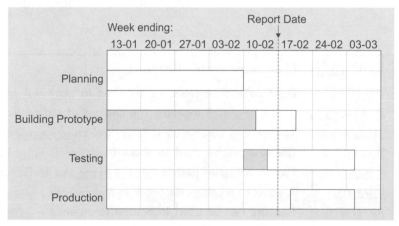

Told you we should have used this chart — we needed at least 500 more slaves...

I Gantt be bothered with this...

Well, it's dull as ditchwater, but... no, actually it <u>is</u> dull as ditchwater. I'm not going to lie to you. Why should you be kept in the dark... makes me sick all this "make it sound interesting" malarkey — if it's boring, I'll jolly well say so — don't you try to stop me, oh no, I'll be speaking to my MP...

Measurement — Data Logging

The stuff in this section is about different ways of <u>recording</u>, <u>controlling</u> and <u>responding to</u> events, either in the real world or in a <u>model</u> of it. It's all good stuff, I assure you.

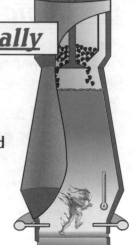

Data Logging means Recording Data Automatically

1) <u>Data logging</u> means <u>capturing</u> and <u>storing</u> information using <u>sensors</u>.

2) The information is first stored as <u>data</u>, and then <u>downloaded</u> into a computer package for analysis.

3) Data logging is best used whenever <u>large amounts</u> of data need to be collected over very <u>long</u> or <u>short</u> periods of time, or from <u>hostile</u> environments.

   Examples of data-logging activities:
   * collecting weather data via <u>satellite</u>,
   * collecting radioactivity data from <u>nuclear power</u> stations,
   * collecting temperature data from inside an <u>oven</u>.

Data Logging needs the Right Hardware and Software

1) Data is collected by an <u>input sensor</u>. Most sensors work by converting environmental signals into <u>electrical</u> energy — producing either an <u>analogue</u> or a <u>digital</u> signal.

2) <u>Digital sensors</u> can usually only be ON or OFF.
   e.g. a pressure pad at a set of traffic lights — it produces a signal when a vehicle drives over it.

3) <u>Analogue sensors</u> can take a range of values.
   E.g. a thermistor — it's a resistor whose resistance changes with temperature.

4) Before an <u>analogue</u> signal can be downloaded and stored on a computer system, it needs to be converted into a <u>digital</u> signal — using an <u>analogue-to-digital converter</u> (<u>ADC</u>).

5) The digital data is often stored in <u>CSV</u> (comma-separated variable) format, so it can be <u>exported</u> into a spreadsheet for data analysis. The output from this analysis can be screen-based or paper-based, and will probably include graphs.

<u>EXAMPLES</u> of how sensors are often used...

<u>Light</u>:	Light-dependent resistors are used to work out when to switch <u>street lights</u> on.
<u>Radioactivity</u>:	<u>Geiger counters</u> measure the amount of radioactivity in an object.
<u>Temperature</u>:	Thermistors can be used to control an <u>air-conditioning system</u>.
<u>Sound</u>:	Sensors can be used to check that <u>aircraft noise</u> keeps within agreed levels.
<u>Pressure</u>:	Like in pressure pads in <u>burglar-alarms</u> or traffic-control systems.
<u>Infra-red</u>:	A sensor can detect a break in an <u>infra-red beam</u> — burglar alarms again.
<u>Air pressure</u>:	Sensors can be used to control emergency <u>oxygen masks</u> on aircraft.

um...

Let's see if you can make sensor this...

Make sure you learn what data logging is, what hardware and software is needed, the difference between analogue and digital signals, and what sensors can measure. Yep — learn it <u>all</u>.

Logging Period and Logging Interval

This stuff's just common sense — but that doesn't mean you don't have to bother learning it.
Make sure you know how to decide on a suitable logging period and logging interval.

Choose an Appropriate Logging Period...

1) The logging period is just the total length of time you're going to collect data for. If it's too long, you can waste valuable time. But if it's too short, you might miss some important data.

2) The logging period depends on the thing that's being monitored.
E.g. if you're investigating the cooling of a cup of coffee, you shouldn't take measurements over a two-year period — one hour would be better.

3) If you're not sure what logging period to use, do some preliminary research — for example, leave a cup of coffee and see roughly how long it takes.

...and a Logging Interval

1) The logging interval is the time between one measurement and the next.

2) As a general rule, the longer the logging period, the longer the logging interval can be.

USE A LONG LOGGING INTERVAL...
If you're measuring the growth of a tree over a two-year period, you could probably have a logging interval of a month.

USE A SHORT LOGGING INTERVAL...
If you were measuring the temperature of a chemical reaction lasting only a couple of seconds, you'd probably want a logging interval of a fraction of a second.

3) Once you've decided on a logging period and logging interval, you can work out the number of readings you'll have — be careful not to make this too small.

$$\text{Number of readings} = \frac{\text{Logging period}}{\text{Logging interval}}$$

Data Logging has Four Benefits

1) Data logging can record information in places where humans find it hard to operate — e.g. the bottom of the sea, outer space, and inside nuclear reactors or pizza ovens.

2) Data can be collected over very long or very short periods — you could record the growth rate of a tree, or the rapidly changing temperature inside a nuclear explosion.

3) Intervals between measurements can be more accurate than when a human's doing the measuring — for example a temperature reading taken every 27 seconds will be exactly that.

4) Data loggers don't need tea breaks, lunch breaks or sleep.
They can even work during Neighbours.

Data logging — look there's just nothing funny to say...

The key things to learn about data logging are the different types of sensor, what information can be collected, the logging period and the logging interval. Just learn that lot and you've got it cracked.

Measuring Physical Data

OK, so computers are great for <u>recording measurements</u>, ya de ya de ya. But you have to <u>plan</u> what you're doing first — loads of <u>fancy sensors</u> measuring the <u>wrong</u> thing is <u>no use</u> whatsoever.

Ask Yourself SIX Questions Before You Start...

1) **Is there more than one change occurring?**

Are you just measuring, say, sound levels? Do you need two things recorded simultaneously?

2) **Is it a sequence of events?**

Are you measuring one thing continuously, or are you measuring the effect of different events on, say, temperature?

3) **Is it a unique event?**

Are you measuring the temperature during a volcanic eruption (unique) or noise levels every time a car goes past (not unique)?

4) **How long will the measurement take?**

Don't plan on measuring the increase in height of an oak tree over 10 minutes. See P.55 for the stuff on logging periods.

5) **How often does the measurement need to be taken?**

This is the stuff on logging intervals (P.55) — you don't want to miss all the changes because you made the interval too big, and you don't want to waste time taking loads of very similar measurements because you're taking measurements too often.

6) **What format do you want the data in?**

You need to think what kind of graph or table you want to produce at the end — some software can output the results straight into a graph of your choice (read on...)

Some Software can Produce Graphs from Sensors

There are some really <u>groovy</u> pieces of software that <u>automatically</u> produce <u>graphs of the data</u> as it's being measured.

These graphs were produced using 'Sensing Science' by Data Harvest. (Pretty groovy, you have to admit.)

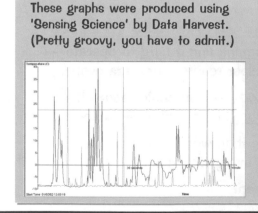
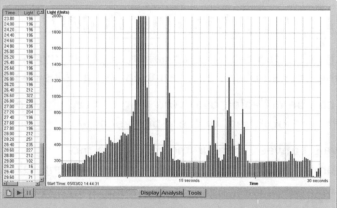

Six questions — I'd rather take the £2000...

You need to understand the importance of planning what you're going to measure before you start. It's all too tempting to get carried away and start measuring the most obvious thing, but mark my words you'll be sorry if you do... and yes I do know I'm ranting — do I look like I care...

Computers and the Law

Computers are increasingly used to <u>store and process important data</u>.
It's very <u>easy</u> to <u>transfer data electronically</u> — so there are <u>laws</u> to control computer use.

The Data Protection Act controls the Use of Personal Data

1) The <u>Data Protection Act</u> gives rights to <u>anyone</u> who has data about them stored on computer.

2) The law allows people to <u>see the personal data</u> stored about them.

3) The Act mainly consists of <u>eight</u> data protection <u>principles</u>. You don't need to learn them, but it's worth knowing roughly what it's about.

Breaking this law can lead to a <u>fine</u> and being made to pay <u>compensation</u>.

Er...your Honour...your wig...it's...um...

Data Protection Act

1 Data must <u>not be processed</u> unless there is a specific <u>lawful reason</u> to do so.

2 Data must <u>only</u> be obtained and then used for <u>specified purposes</u>.

3 Data should be <u>adequate</u>, <u>relevant</u>, and <u>not excessive</u> for the specified use.

4 Data must be <u>accurate</u> and, where relevant, kept <u>up to date</u>.

5 Data should only be kept <u>as long as it's needed</u> for the specified purpose.

6 Data processing should meet the <u>legal rights</u> of the people concerned.

7 Data holders should <u>protect the data</u> against loss, theft or corruption.

8 Data should <u>not be transferred abroad</u>, except to certain other European countries.

The Copyright, Design and Patents Act controls Illegal Copying

This law makes it <u>illegal to copy a file</u> without the <u>permission</u> of the <u>owner</u> or <u>copyright holder</u>.
There are <u>four ways</u> the law is often broken:

1) <u>Using software</u> without the proper <u>licence</u>. So if you have a software licence for one computer, but you then install it on all the machines in a <u>network</u>, you're breaking the law.

2) <u>Downloading</u> text or images <u>from the internet</u> and <u>using</u> them without saying where you got them, or without receiving the copyright owner's <u>permission</u>.

3) <u>Copying</u> a computer program you use at work and running it on a computer at home, without <u>permission</u> from the copyright holder.

People who break this law risk an <u>unlimited</u> fine.

4) Making <u>copies</u> of software and giving it to your <u>friends</u>.

The Computer Misuse Act prevents Illegal Access to Files

This law deals with the problems of computer <u>hackers</u> and <u>viruses</u> — it made <u>three things illegal</u>:

1) <u>Unauthorised access</u> to <u>computer material</u> (e.g. <u>hacking</u>). This includes viewing parts of a network you're not permitted to see, and the illegal copying of programs — <u>software piracy</u>.

2) Gaining <u>unauthorised access</u> to a computer to carry out serious <u>crimes</u> like <u>fraud</u> and <u>blackmail</u>.

Oi — you're nicked...

3) <u>Unauthorised changing</u> of computer files — including <u>planting viruses</u>, and <u>deleting files</u>.

An offender can face an <u>unlimited fine</u> and a <u>five-year</u> prison <u>sentence</u>.

The most exciting page in the world ever — probably...

There's a lot of boring information on this page. Soz, like.

Computers and the Workplace

ICT is changing the <u>types of jobs</u> that people do. It's not just the <u>electronic office</u> either — read on...

ICT has Replaced Some Jobs but Created Others

Computers have completely <u>replaced</u> humans in some jobs, and meant that <u>fewer</u> people are needed to do others. But <u>new jobs</u> have been created in <u>building and operating computers</u> and <u>new industries</u> have emerged.

JOBS BEING REPLACED BY COMPUTERS

1) <u>Manual jobs</u> replaced by <u>robots</u>, e.g. some car-assembly jobs.

2) <u>Manual jobs</u> replaced by <u>computer systems</u>, e.g. manual print-workers replaced by DTP.

3) <u>Office jobs</u> replaced by <u>computers</u>, e.g. filing clerks and typists.

JOBS BEING CREATED BY COMPUTERS

1) Jobs involved in the <u>design</u> and <u>manufacture</u> of computer hardware.

2) <u>Systems analysts</u> and <u>programmers</u> to design systems and write software.

3) <u>Network managers</u> and <u>technicians</u> to maintain computer systems.

ICT enables Teleworking and Hot-Desking

1) Internet technology means employees can <u>telework</u> (i.e. work from home) instead of going in to the office.

2) <u>Hot-desking</u> is when an employee sits at any free desk in an office, rather than having their own special place.

Teleworking means you can work anywhere you want.

ADVANTAGES

1) Less <u>office space</u> needed.

2) Teleworking employees spend <u>less time commuting</u> and can organise work around their <u>personal life</u>.

DISADVANTAGES

1) Harder to keep information <u>confidential</u>.

2) Teleworking can be <u>lonely</u> (less contact with colleagues).

3) Hot-desking can be <u>stressful</u> — never knowing where you'll be sitting.

ICT is increasingly used by All Workers

<u>Workers</u> in general, and particularly those in <u>office jobs</u>, are being required to spend <u>more and more</u> of their working day <u>using computers</u>. This has <u>pros</u> and <u>cons</u> for both employers and employees:

COMPUTERS ARE GREAT BECAUSE:

1) Computers can <u>increase</u> the amount of work done. This makes businesses more <u>productive</u> and so more <u>competitive</u>.

2) Computers can do the <u>boring</u>, <u>repetitive</u> work and leave employees to do the <u>interesting jobs</u>.

COMPUTERS ARE PANTS BECAUSE:

1) It's <u>expensive</u> to keep investing in the latest and most efficient technology and it takes <u>time and money</u> to <u>retrain</u> staff.

2) There may be <u>job losses</u> as <u>computers replace people</u> for some tasks.

3) Continued use of computers can cause <u>health problems</u> (see next page).

ICT is everywhere — everywhere I tell you...

Pretty much <u>whatever job</u> you do, you'll have to <u>use a computer</u> at some point. Which is quite odd, given that only 30 years ago, you'd probably <u>never</u> use a computer — no matter what job you did.

Computer Use — Health and Safety Issues

Computers weren't originally designed to be used all day — people who do use them a lot are at risk of injury. This page isn't much fun, but it's not meant to be — this is seriously important stuff.

The Main Problems are RSI, Eye Strain and Fitness...

There are three main problems — connected with poor design of the equipment, not using the equipment properly or overusing it.

1) Repetitive strain injury (RSI) is a general term for muscle or tendon damage with chronic aches and pains, resulting from overuse of a keyboard or mouse.
2) Spending too long in front of a VDU can cause eye strain and headaches.
3) Circulation, fitness and back problems might result from sitting all day in front of a computer rather than walking around.

...Which have Three Main Solutions

1) Take regular breaks from computer work. Looking away from the screen, walking around and exercising your fingers and hands can also help to reduce the health risks.
2) Use the correct equipment. You should have:
   a) a proper computer chair with backrest,
   b) a good, well-positioned keyboard that makes typing less of a strain on fingers.
   c) good background lighting,
   d) a screen filter (if necessary) to reduce VDU glare,
   Things like wrist rests for the keyboard and mouse can also help.
3) Arrange the equipment properly. Adjust the chair and VDU to find the most comfortable position.

How to Sit Properly at Your Computer: You should have a chair with a backrest. Your feet should touch the floor (if they don't, you need a footrest or a lower chair and desk). Your eyes should be level with the top of the VDU. Your forearms should be roughly horizontal (keeping the wrists straight is the main thing). This might not be perfect for everyone, but it's a good general rule.

And how not to do it...

There's a Health and Safety Law to Protect Employees

The law says that employers need to do five main things to protect their workers:
1) Check that computer equipment and the work area is safe.
2) Ensure workstations meet minimum requirements (including everything from chairs to lighting).
3) Employers must provide regular breaks or allow employees to do non-computer work.
4) Provide free eye-tests for all staff who regularly use VDUs in their job.
5) Provide health and safety training and information, so people can reduce the risks.

Suddenly lion taming doesn't seem so bad after all...

Hey ho. Not the most jolly page, but an important one. Basically if you get any aches and pains then you're doing something wrong. Work out what it is and do something about it (or you'll regret it later...)

Revision Summary for Section Seven

OK, last section of the book, biggest list of questions. Ahahahahahaha...

1) What's a bar code, and what's it used for?

2) What does EPOS stand for?

3) Explain how an EPOS system can automatically reorder stock.

4) What does EFTPOS stand for?

5) How can the risk of card fraud be reduced?

6) Explain one reason why retailers have introduced loyalty cards.

7) What's a "car park management system" and how does it work?

8) What's ICT got to do with weather forecasting? Explain briefly what it's all about.

9) What's a "point of information"? Name one place where you've seen one.

10) What's a Gantt diagram?
    a)   a drawing of a bird
    b)   a project management tool
    c)   a bus timetable

11) Give a definition of data logging.

12) What's the difference between analogue and digital sensors?

13) Give <u>three</u> examples of types of sensors and give one possible use for each.

14) Explain the difference between a logging period and a logging interval.

15) Give <u>three</u> benefits of using data logging.

16) When you're measuring something with sensors, should you plan what you're doing first? Why/why not?

17) Write down <u>two</u> questions you might ask yourself before you start measuring.

18) What's the Data Protection Act for (briefly)?

19) Which of these are legal?
    — Buying a PC game and making copies of it for your mates
    — Buying a game and using it on your home PC
    — Writing a virus program and e-mailing it to the Whitehouse
    — Downloading a picture and getting permission from the copyright owner to use it on your own website
    — Hacking into government files and changing every 13th word to "Tony".

20) Name two jobs being replaced by computers and two jobs being created by computers.

21) Explain teleworking and hotdesking.

22) Give one benefit and one disadvantage to a business of using computers.

23) List all of the health problems you can think of that can be caused by overuse of computers, and ways of avoiding each of them.

Index

Symbols

80s hair 24

A

absolute cell references 34
access rights 4
access security 4
ace time-saving tip 20
adc (analogue-to-digital
        converter) 54
address book 49
Adobe Photoshop 26
aligning text 21
analogue sensors 54
Andy 23
animated gifs 46
animation effects 30
applications software 23
archiving 4
attachments 48
automatic data capture 8

B

back-up 4
bacon-double-turnip burger 5
bar code 6, 51
bar graphs 35
bar code reader 8
batch processing 11
biased information 43
big boss 29
binary code 1
bitmaps 6, 24
bits 1
body odour 22
body text 29
bold type 21, 44
bookmarks 41
borders 21, 22
Boris 11
brightness 26
Britney 26
browser 39
bullet points 21, 30
burglar alarms 6, 54
byline 29
bytes 1

C

calculators 33
capturing data 8-9, 10,
            16, 17, 54
car park barriers 18
car park management
        systems 52
card fraud 51
cause and effect 18
CD-ROMs 40
cells 33
characters 11
charts 12, 35
cheese web sites 41
circuits 1
click 5
click and drag 20

clip-art 23, 24
codes 16, 37
colouring images 25
colouring text 21
columns 22, 28
commands 16
communicating
        information 30, 35
complex controls 10
computer modelling 52
computer misuse act 57
computer systems 2, 3
concept keyboards 5
constraints of the system 15
contrast 26
control systems 18
coordinates 35
copy and paste 20
copying files 3
copyright 24, 47, 57
Corel Photopaint 26
corrupt files 10
counters 18
CPU (Central Processing Unit) 2
creating images 24
credit cards 6
cropping images 25
CSV (Comma-Separated Variable)
        54
ctrl (or "control") key 20
cursor 5
cursor keys 20
customer database 52
cut and paste 20
CVs 23

D

Daley Thompson's pants 28
data 1, 2, 6, 8-12, 16, 33-36, 37,
        52, 54-56
data capture 8, 9, 10, 16, 17
data entering 5
data files 11
data logging 54
data presentation 12
data protection act 57
data security 4
data storage 10
data validation 16
database 23
    fields 37
    key field 37
    records 37
deadline 29
debit card 51
deleting text 20
designing a computer system 16-17
desktop publishing (DTP) 27-29, 58
diagrams 17
digital signals 54
digital cameras 6, 24
digital sensors 54
display panel 5
distorted graphics 25
distribution lists 49

double click 5, 20
double-line spacing 21
dpi (dots per inch) 24
drawing software 24
DTP (Desktop Publishing) 27-29, 58

E

e-mail (electronic mail) 39, 48
    attachments 6
    client 39
editing digital images 26
editor 29
EFTPOS (Electronic Funds Transfer
        at the Point of Sale) 51
electricity-meter-reading
        forms 8
electronic kiosks 53
electronic mail 48
embedding objects into documents
        23
envelopes 23
EPOS (Electronic Point of Sale) 51
evaluation 18
export 25
eye strain 59

F

fake photos 26
favourites 41
fax machine 6
feasibility study 15
feedback loops 2
fields 11, 37
file attachments 48
file format 23
file size 24
filters 26
fish fingers 21
fitness 59
Five Golden Rules 44
fixed-length fields 11
flat-bed scanners 6
flow diagrams 17
font 21
footers 22
forearms 59
formatting toolbar 21
forms 8, 9, 16
formulas 34
frames 27, 28, 46
fraud 57
fun 26
functions 34

G

Gantt diagram 53
gas-flooding systems 4
Gb (gigabyte) 1
geiger counters 54
gif pictures 45
GIGO 1
GIS (geographical information
        systems) 52
graphics 24-25, 26,
        27-29, 44-46
graphics pads 5

graphics software 24, 25
graphics tablets 5
graphs 12, 23, 35, 36, 56
grouping images 25
guidelines 28

H

hackers 3, 10, 57
handles for resizing 25
hard copy 12
hardware 4, 5
headers 22
headline 29
health and safety issues 59
heaven 21
high resolution 6
highlight text 20
history 41
hot-desking 58
house style 29
HTML 46
hue 26
human error 3, 6
hyperlinks 41, 44

I

icons 5
ICT jobs 58
illegal 57
image-doctoring 26
images 24
importing 23, 27
indenting text 21
information 1-3, 6, 8-9, 12, 39-
        43, 51, 53
infra-red sensors 6
input 2, 5, 6, 15
Input, Process, Output 2, 16
internet. *See also* web and www
    Internet Service Provider
        (ISP) 39, 48
italics 21

J

JLo 26
job losses 58
JPEG 24, 45
justified text 21

K

Kb (kilobyte) 1
key field 37
key points 21
keyboards 5
keywords 40

L

laptops 5
laser scanners 6, 51
laws 57
layered frames 28
layering 25, 26, 28
layout of newspaper 29
layout of page 27, 28
leaflets 27
legend 35

Index

letter template 23
licenced software 57
light pens 6
light sensors 6
line graphs 35
line spacing 21
linked frames 28
links 46
logging interval 55-56
logging period 55-56
lonely 60
loyalty cards 52

M

magnetic reader 51
magnetic stripe cards 6, 51
mail merge 17, 23
manual jobs replaced by
    computers 58
manual methods 8
manual systems 3
Mb (megabyte) 1
membrane 5
memo 23
microphones 6
mixed cell 33
modelling 36, 52
modem 39
monitoring systems 18
morse code 1
mouse 5
mouse balls 5
moving text 20
multi-page documents 22
multimedia presentations
    12, 30

N

network managers 58
network security 4
news team 29
newsletters 23, 27, 28
newspapers 28, 29
noticeboard 27
numbering 21

O

objectives 15
output 15, 16

P

page footers 22
page guidelines 28
page headers 22

page layout 27, 28
paint spray 25
painting software 24
paperclip 22
passwords 4
paste 20
patient records 17
permission 57
personalised letters 23
personalised mailshots 52
photo-editing software 6
photographer 29
physical data 56
physical security 4
pie charts 35
pimples on laptops 5
pixels 6, 24
pizza 36
plagiarism 47
posters 27
power cut 3
presentation 16
presentation software 30, 31
primary data 43
prison 57
privacy 10
procedures 18
processing 2
processing does it 11
professional looking pages 27
programmers 58
programming 18
proof-read 29
publishing software 27

Q

questionnaires 8-9
QWERTY keyboards 5

R

readability 22
read-only files 4
real-time processing 11
records 11, 37
red raging rhinocerous 22
rejection rate 9
relative cell references 34
repetitive strain injury (RSI) 59
reporter 29
resizing objects 25
resolution 24
rigid stylus 5
robots 58
Ronan Keating 40
rotating objects 25

rules of the system 15

S

SADFLAB 4
scanners 8, 24
    flat-bed 6
    hand-held 6
scatter graphs 35
school canteen 36
screen display 12
screen forms 16
script 31
search engine 40
secondary data 43
security 3, 4
sensors 6, 8, 52, 54
    for mouses 5
serial numbers 4
setting up a computer system 3
sharpness 26
shift key 20
shortcuts 20
simulations 36
single-line spacing 21
slides 30, 31
software piracy 57
sound card 12
spell checker 22
spider chart 47
splash 29
spreadsheets 33
    cells 33
    coordinates 33
    formulas 34
    relative cell references 34
    spreadsheet models 36
standard letter 23
storage medium 4
stressful 60
style sheets 28
subeditor 29
subheading 29
system 2
system failure 3
system flow charts 17
system life cycle 14
systems analysis 14
systems analyst 16, 58

T

tables 22
tables in wordprocessors 22
tasks 16
technicians 58

teleworking 58
temperature sensors 6
templates 23, 28
test plan 16
text frames 27
text wrapping 28
text size 21
thank goodness 29
ticket barriers 18
top-down diagrams 17
touch-screen technology 53
touch-sensitive
    pads 5
tracker balls on laptops 5
traffic lights 18
traffic management 52
triple click 20
turnaround document 8

U

unauthorised
    access 57
    users 3
underlining text 21
underlining 21
undo 20
url 40
user-friendly 16

V

validation 2
variable length fields 11
vector graphics 24
vector-based software 24
verification 2
viruses 10, 48, 57
voice recognition systems 6

W

weather forecasting 52
web browser 39
web design 45
what-if analysis 36
word processing 20, 22, 23.
    See also text editing
workplace 58
workstations 59
wrapping text 28
wrist rests 59
WWW (World Wide Web) 39